Real World

Colouring Book

For Advanced Users & Adults

50 Images

Created From Real Life Photos For You To Colour As You Please.

ISBN 978-0-359-86322-8
90000
9 780359 863228

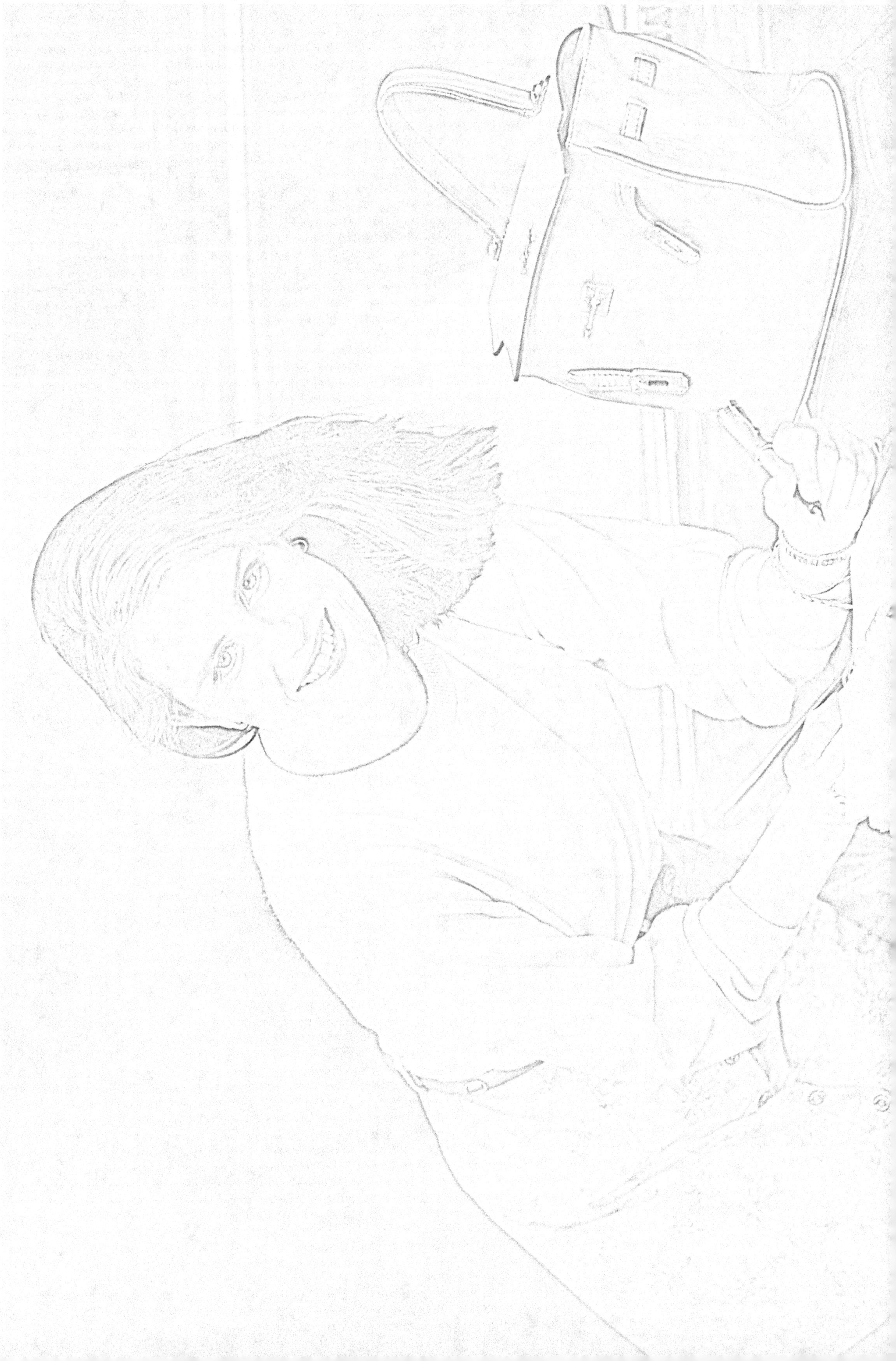

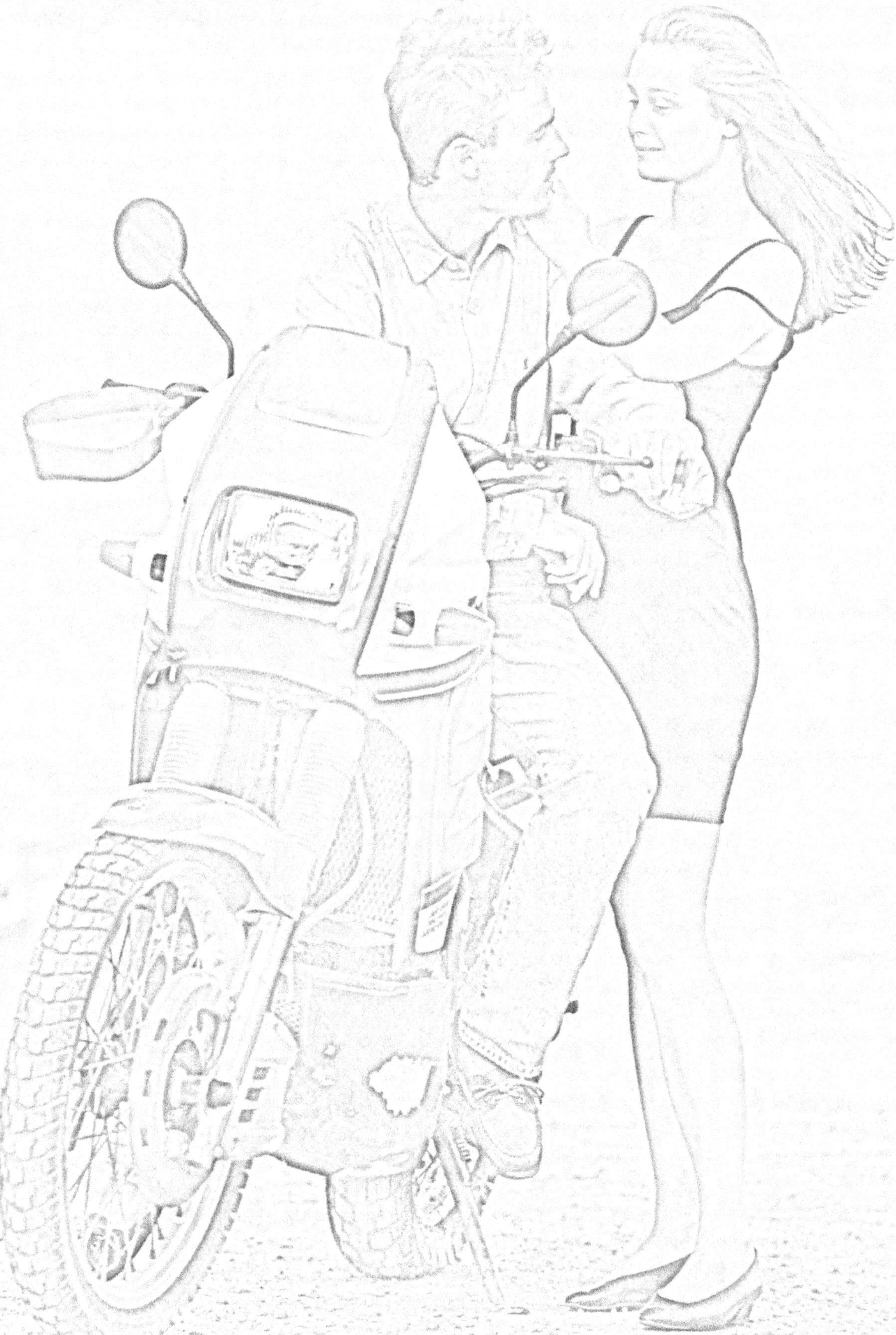

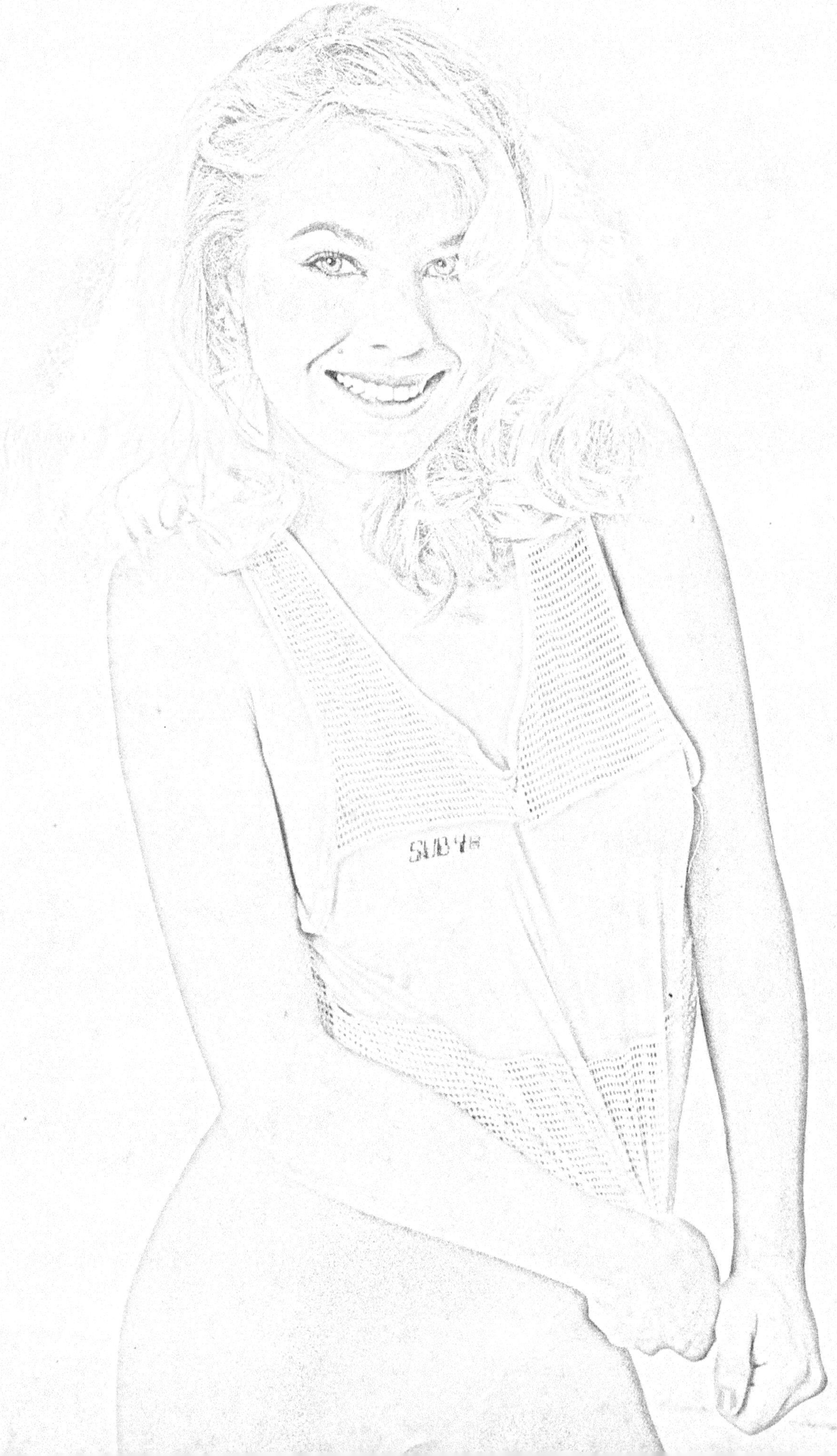

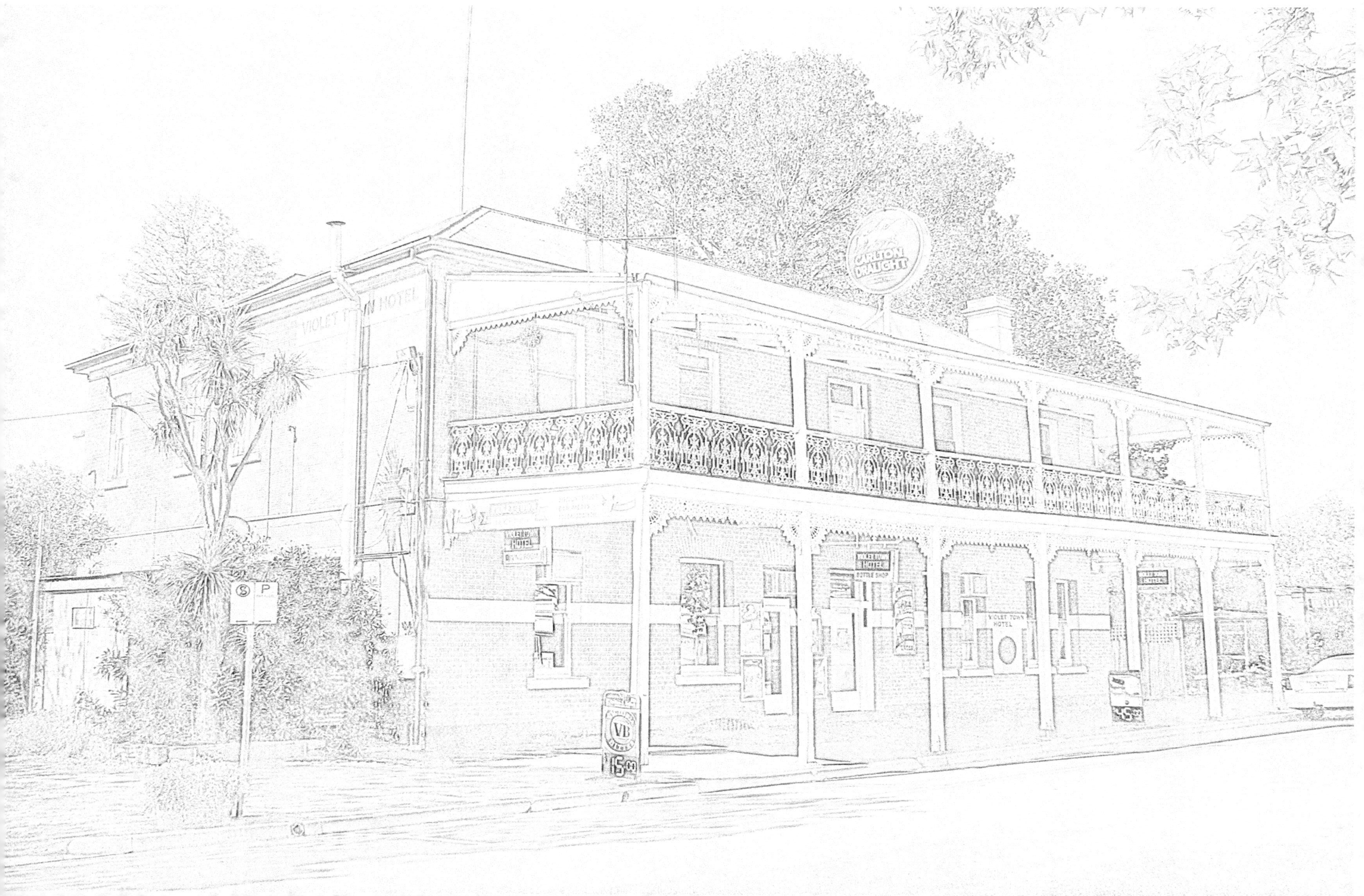
CARLTON DRAUGHT
VIOLET TOWN HOTEL
VIOLET TOWN HOTEL BOTTLE SHOP
VIOLET TOWN HOTEL
VB

POST AND TELEGRAPH OFFICE.
Gloria Jean's Coffees

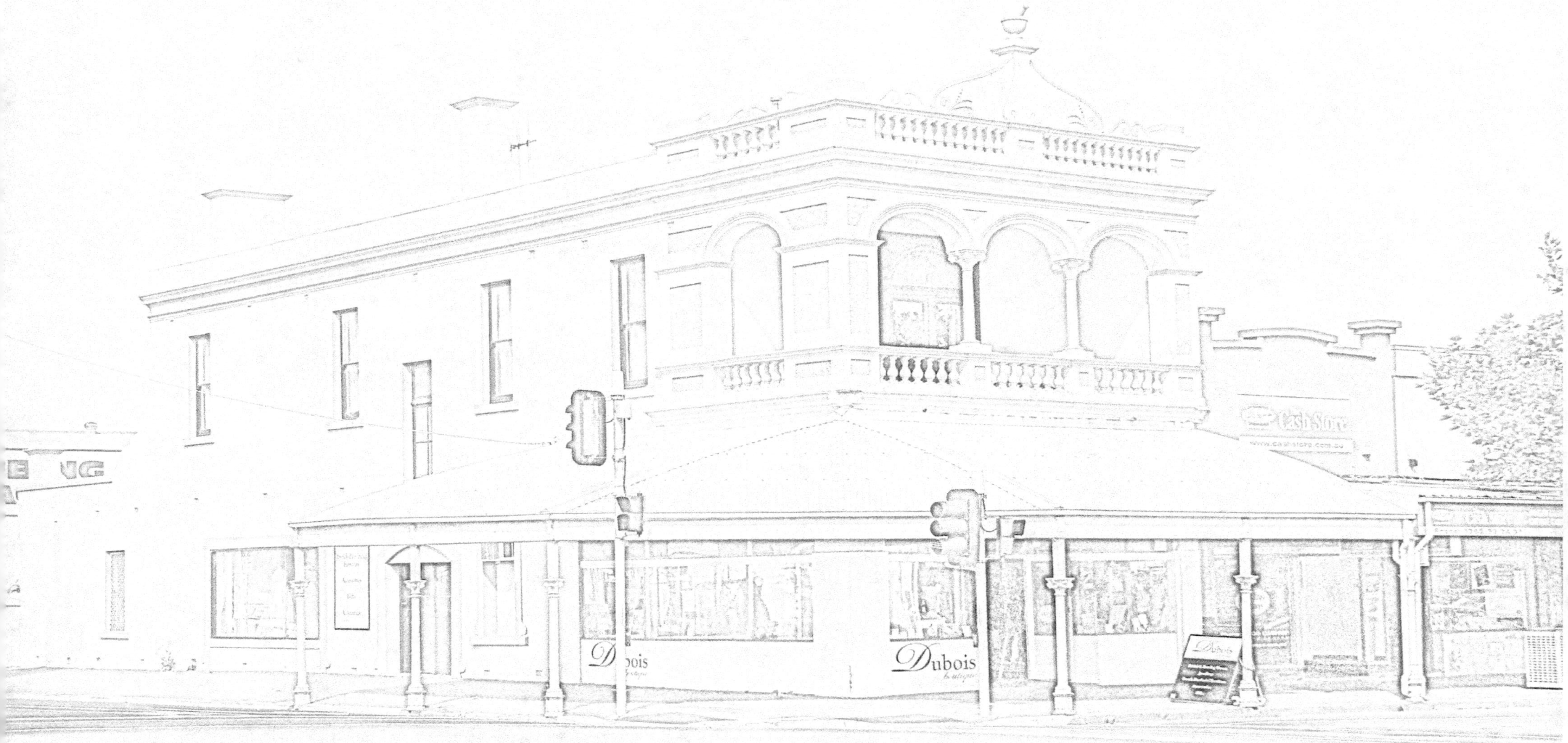
Dubois
Dubois
Dubois
Cash Store

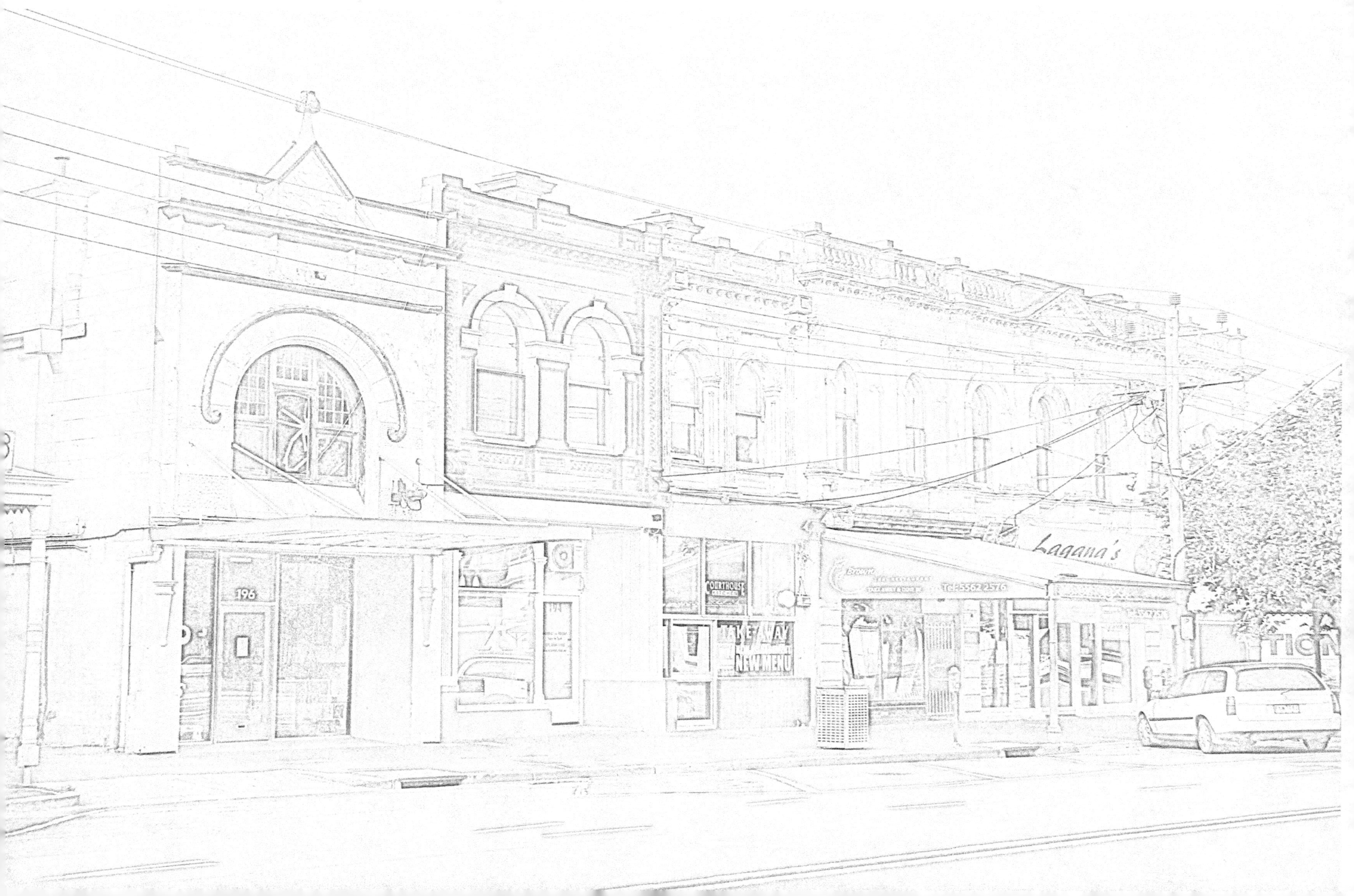
196
COURTHOUSE
TAKE AWAY
NEW MENU
Tel: 5562 2576
Lagana's

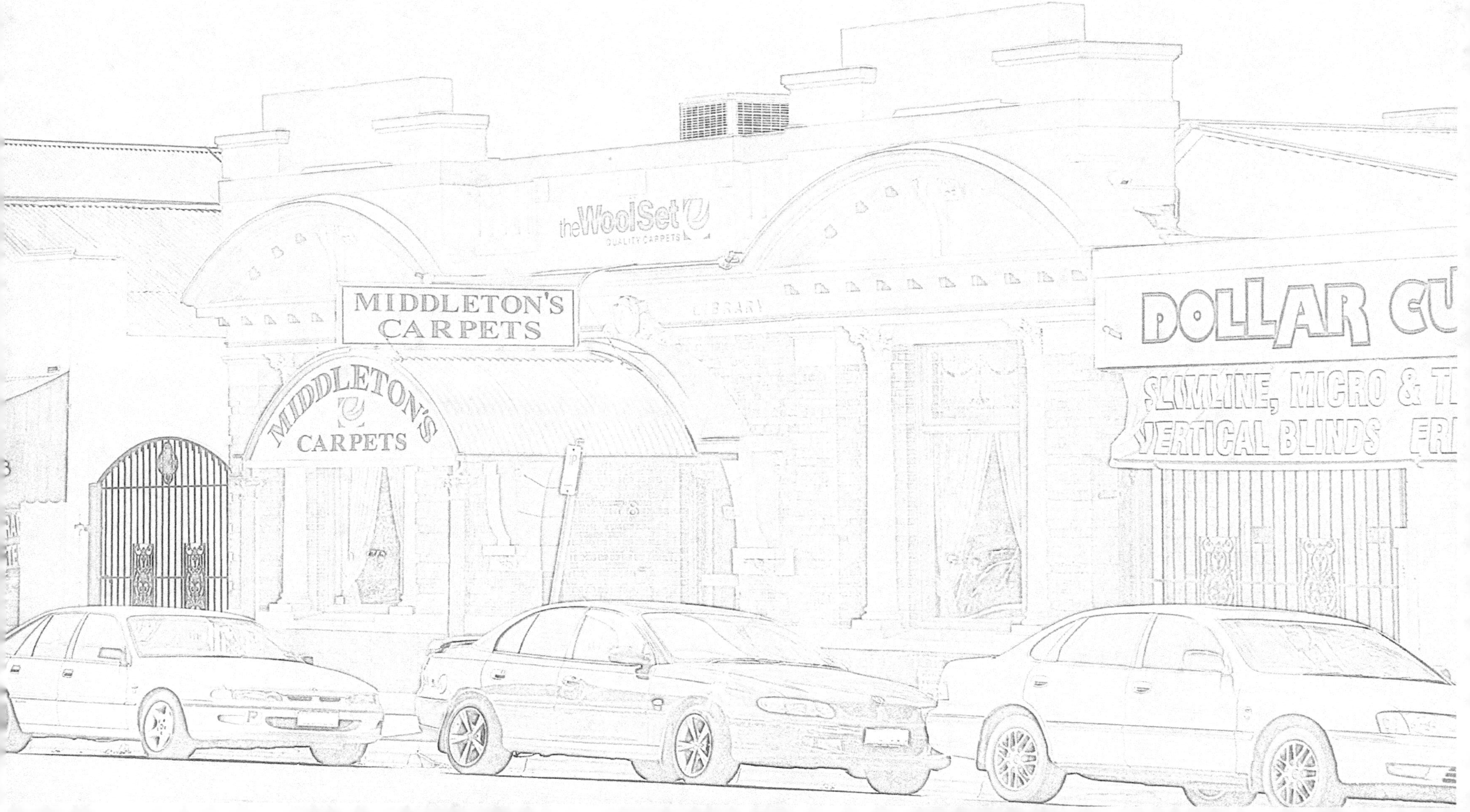
theWoolSet
QUALITY CARPETS
MIDDLETON'S CARPETS
MIDDLETON'S
CARPETS
LIBRARY
DOLLAR
SLIMLINE, MICRO &
VERTICAL BLINDS

CHANTRY FAIRE
FINE CRAFTS & GIFTS
GIFTS
GIFTWARE & FURNITURE
AUSTRALIANA
NATURES SOAPS
COLLECTABLES
FURNITURE
JEWELLERY

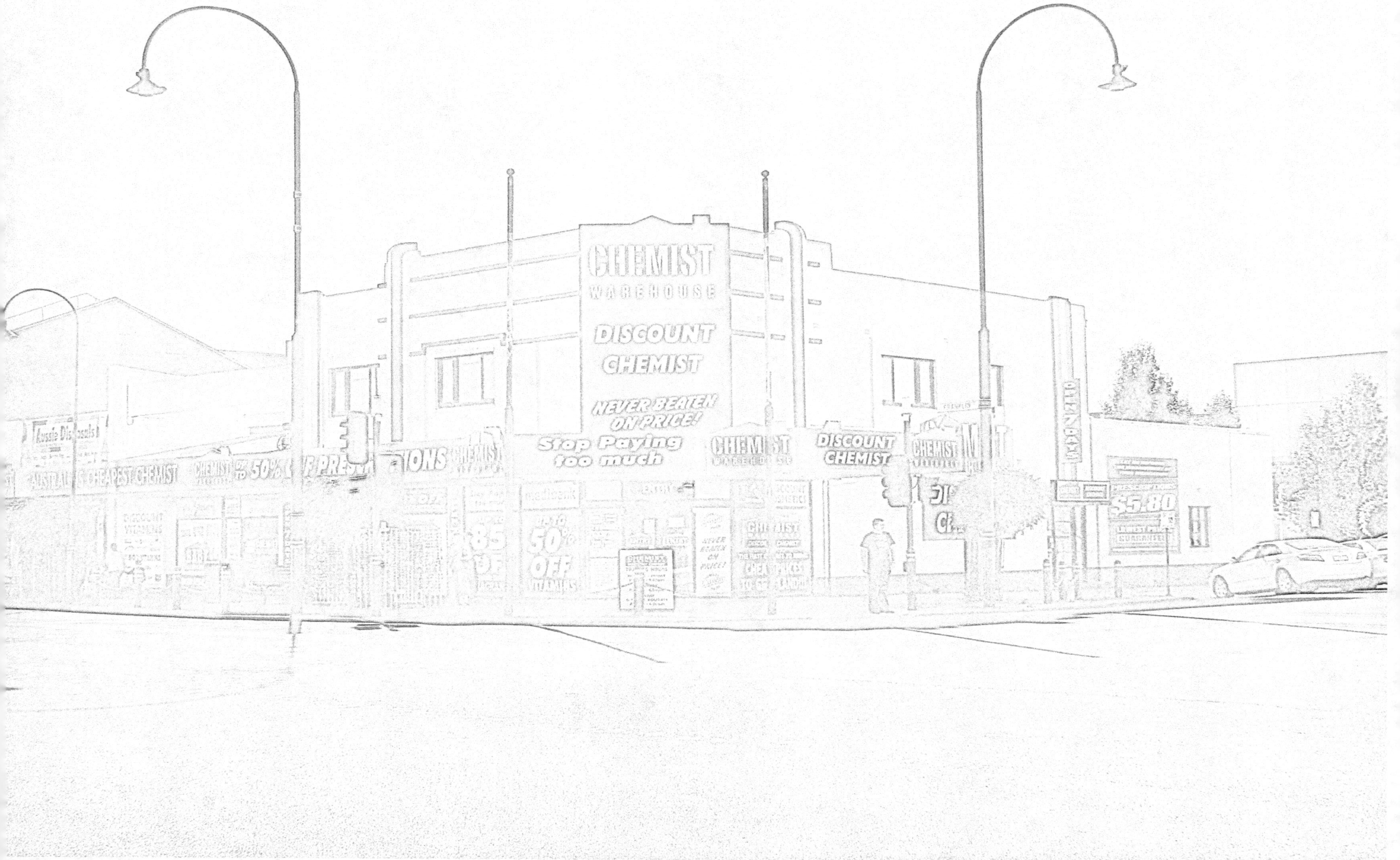

CHEMIST
WAREHOUSE
DISCOUNT
CHEMIST
NEVER BEATEN
ON PRICE!
Stop Paying
too much
CHEMIST
WAREHOUSE
DISCOUNT
CHEMIST
$5.80
UP TO
50%
OFF
VITAMINS

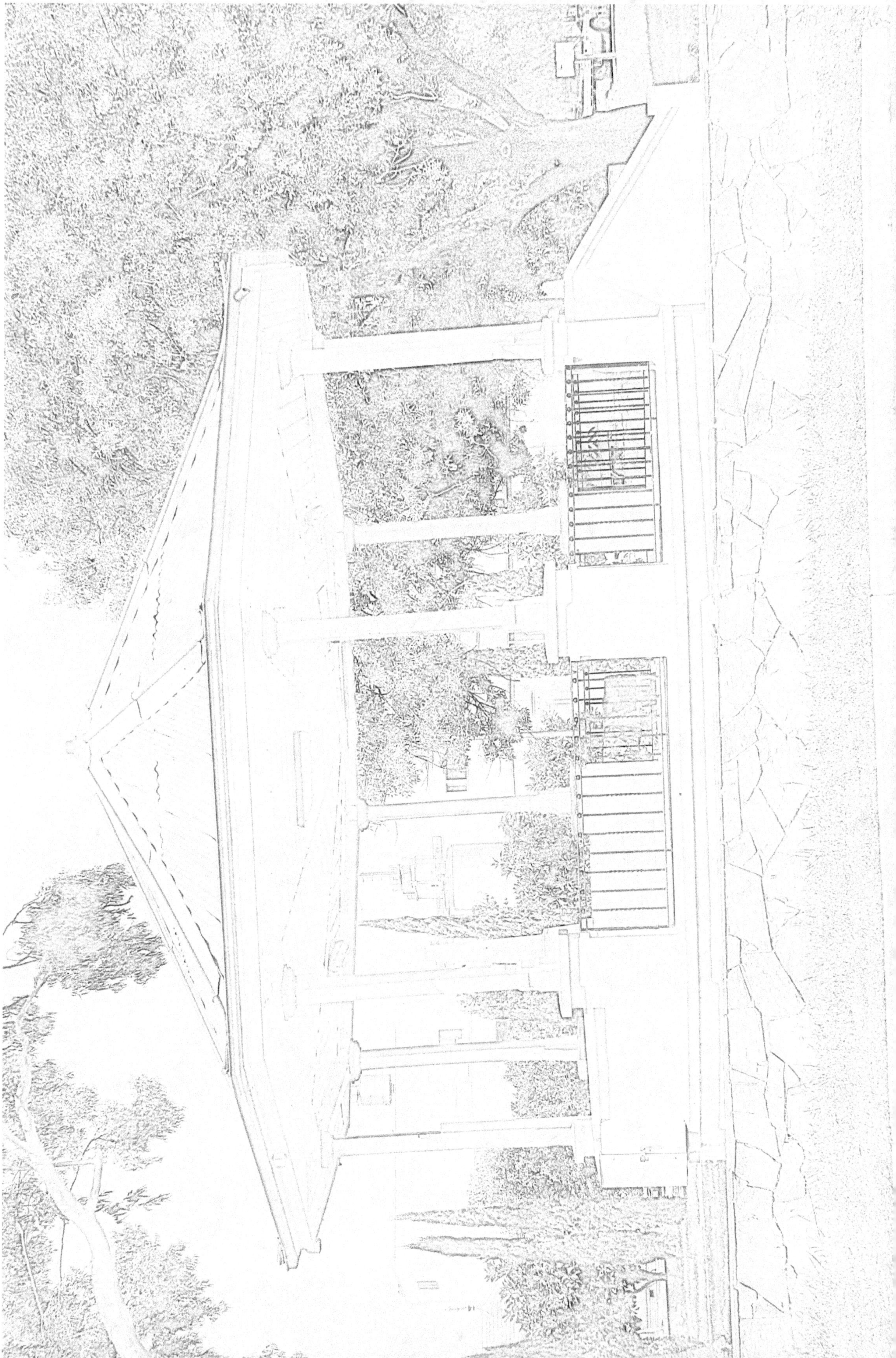

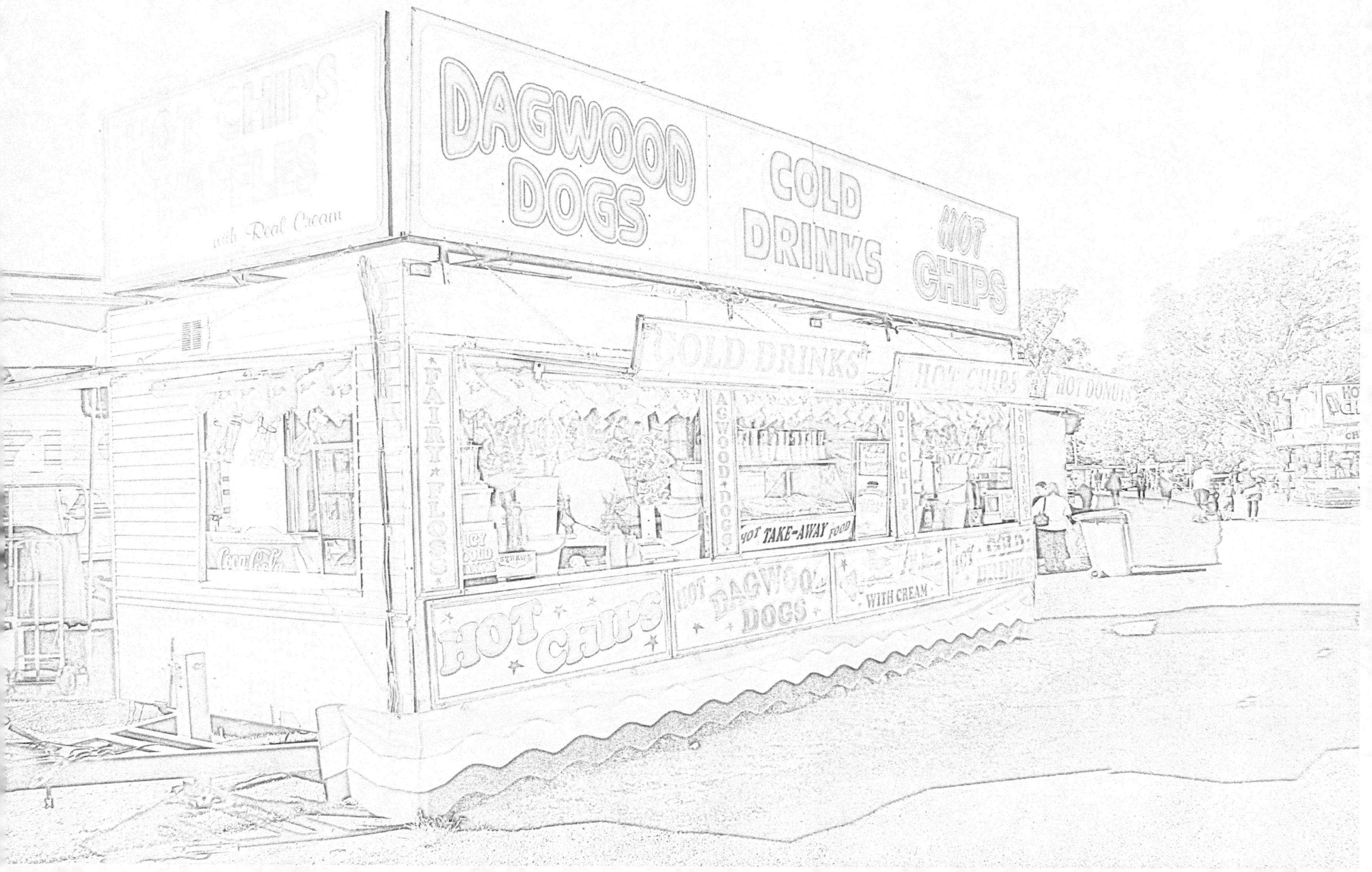
DAGWOOD DOGS
COLD DRINKS
HOT CHIPS
with Real Cream
COLD DRINKS
HOT CHIPS
HOT DONUTS
FAIRY FLOSS
AGWOOD DOGS
HOT TAKE-AWAY FOOD
HOT CHIPS
HOT DAGWOOD DOGS
WITH CREAM
STRAWS
Coca-Cola

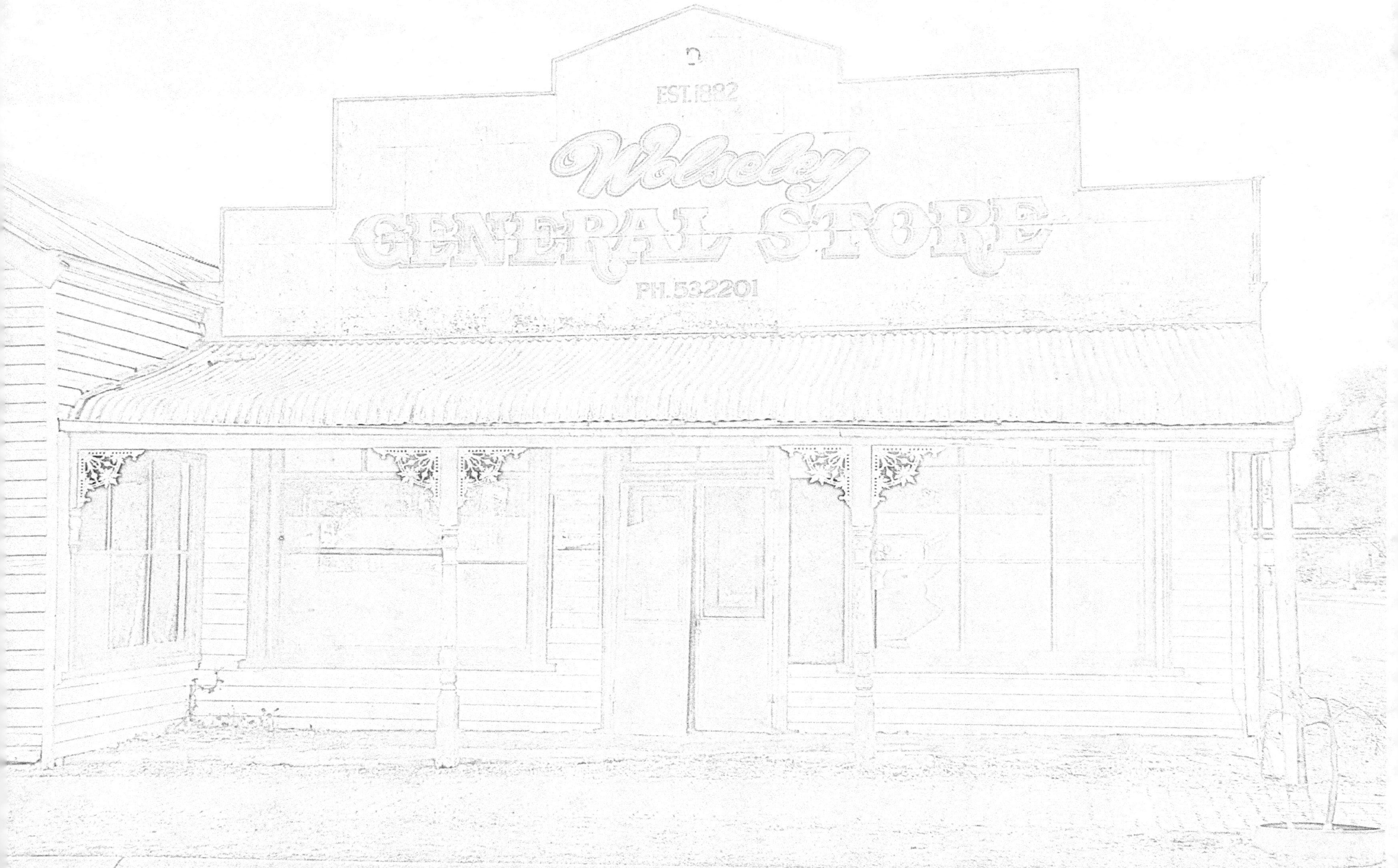
EST. 1882
Wolseley
GENERAL STORE
PH. 532201

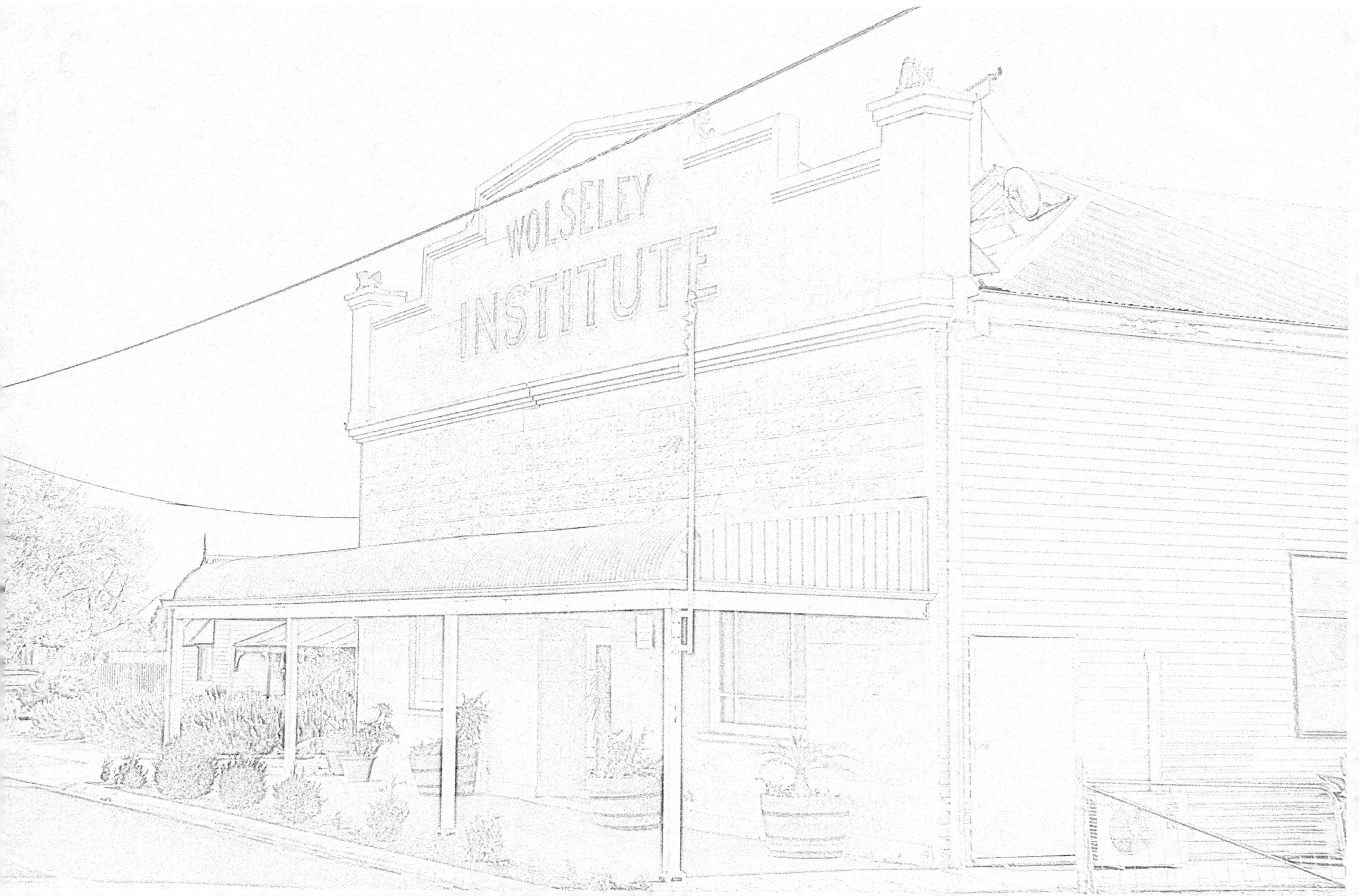
WOLSELEY
INSTITUTE

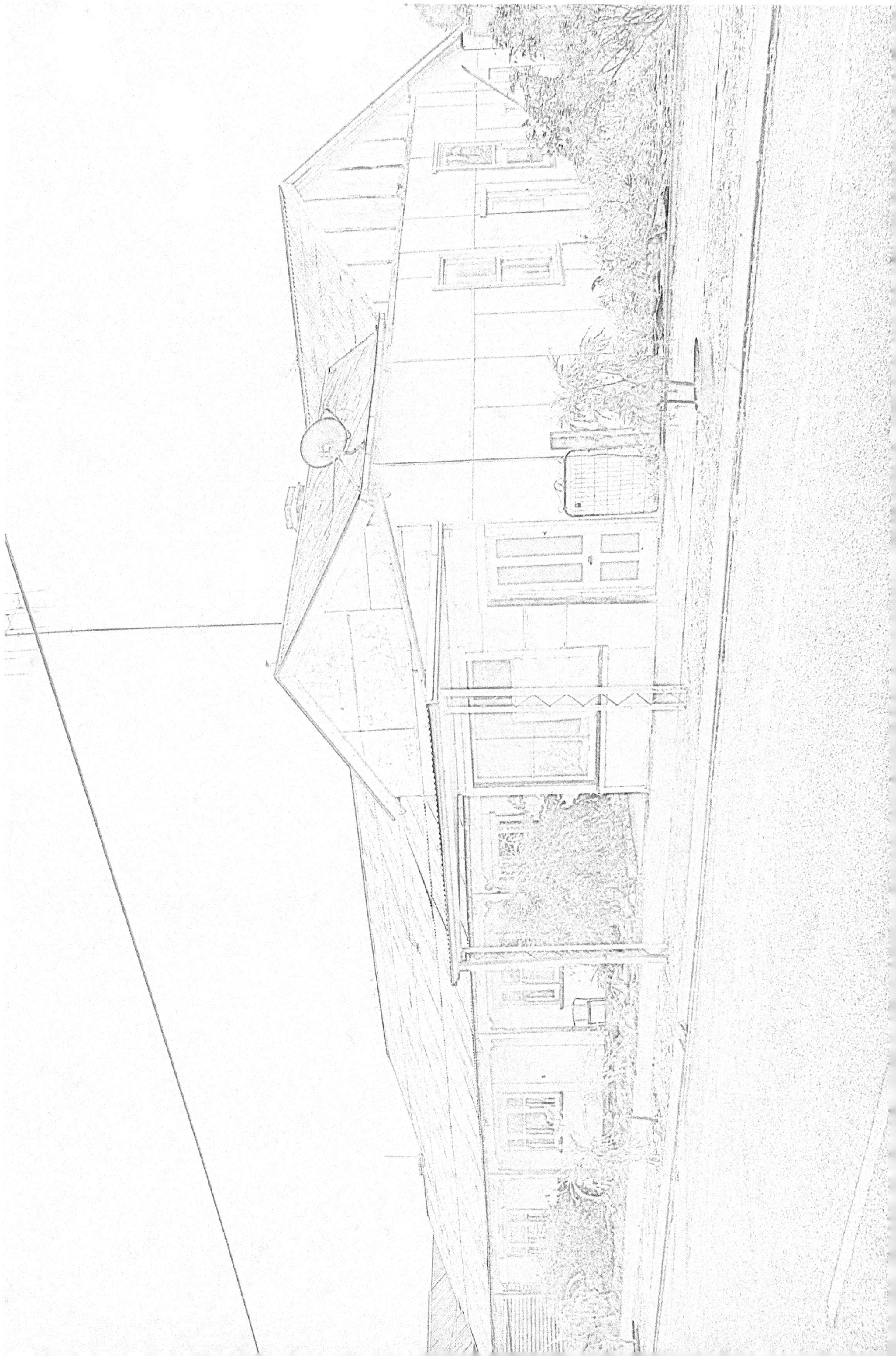

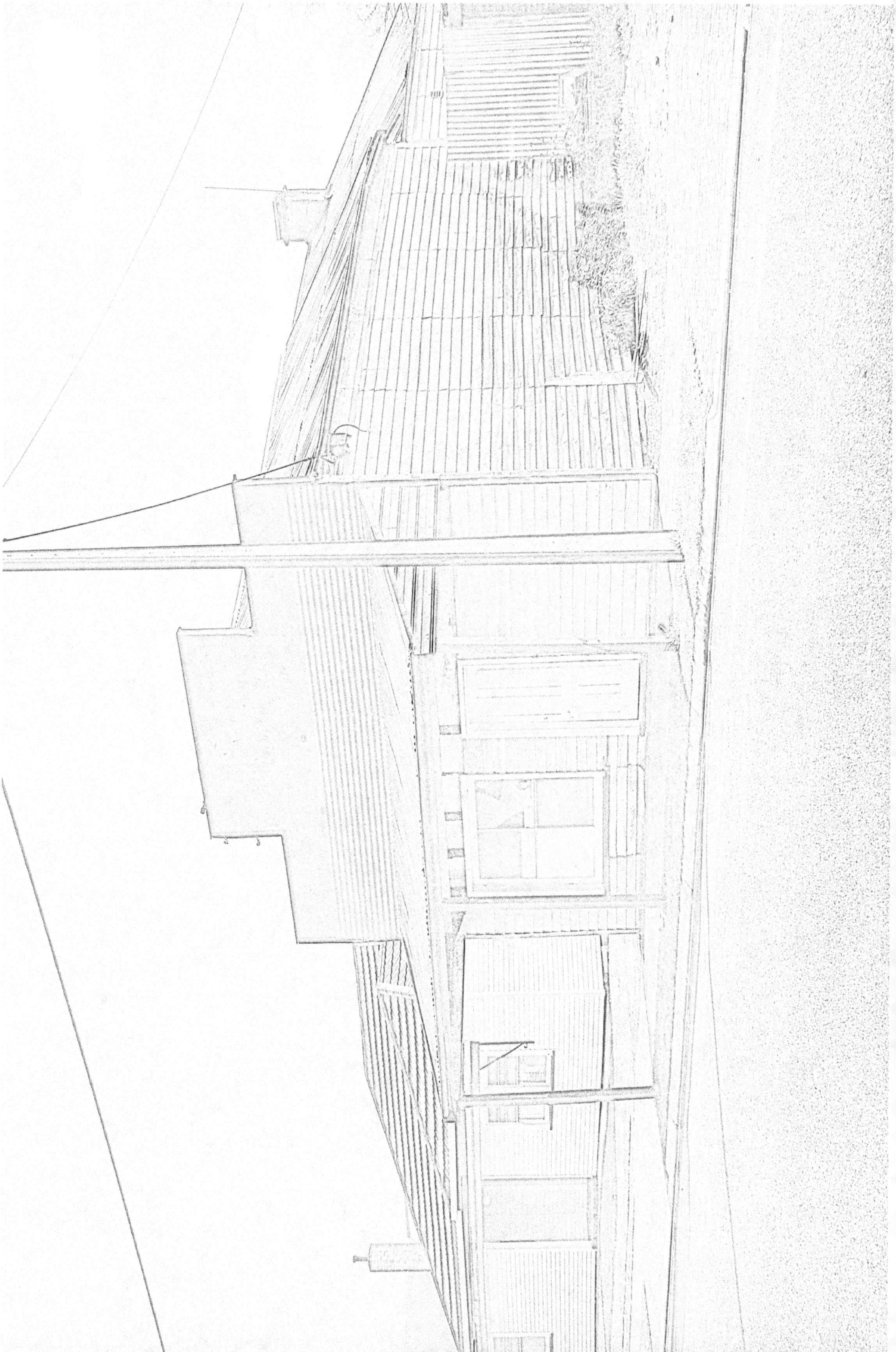

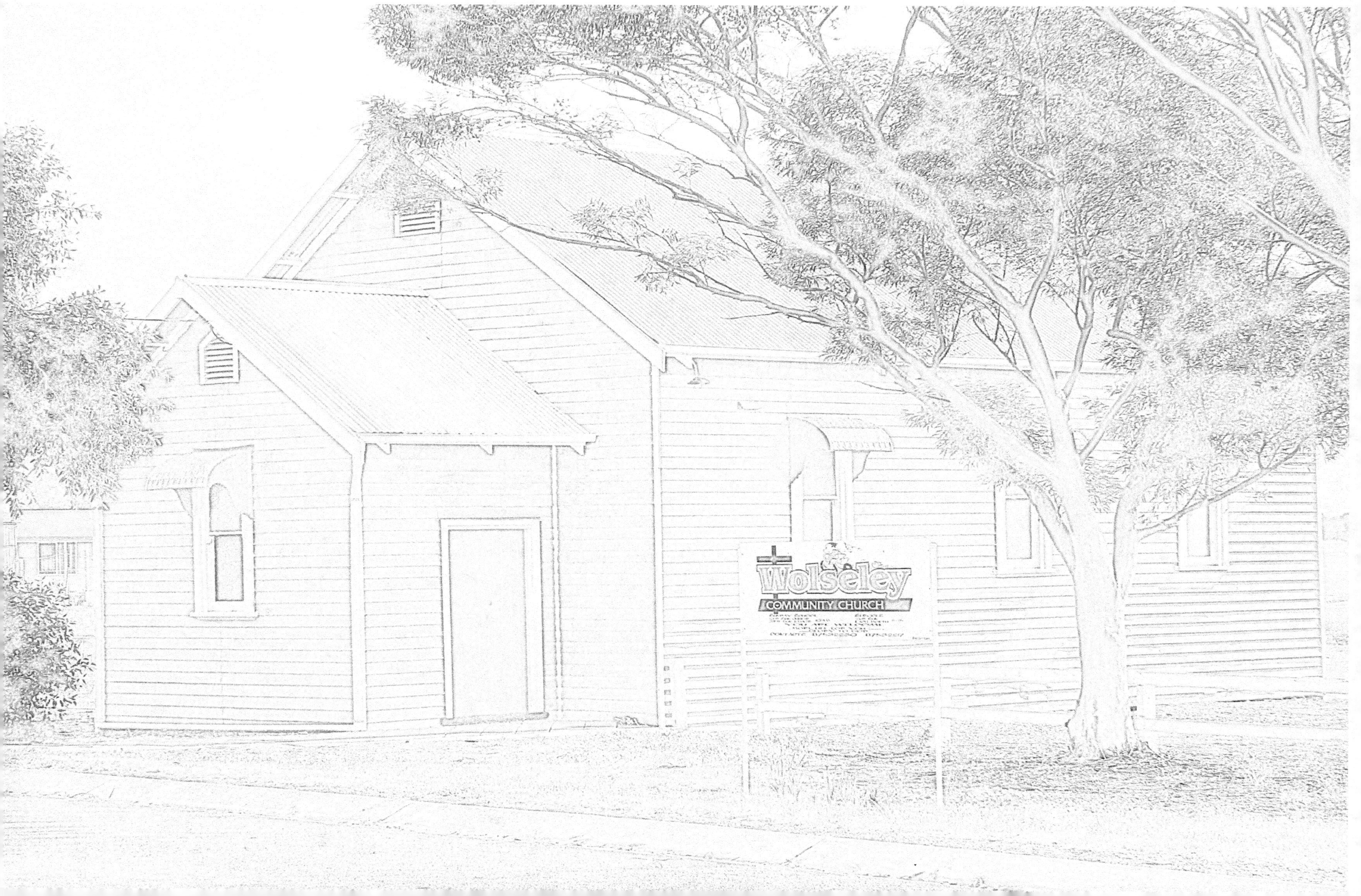
Wolseley
COMMUNITY CHURCH

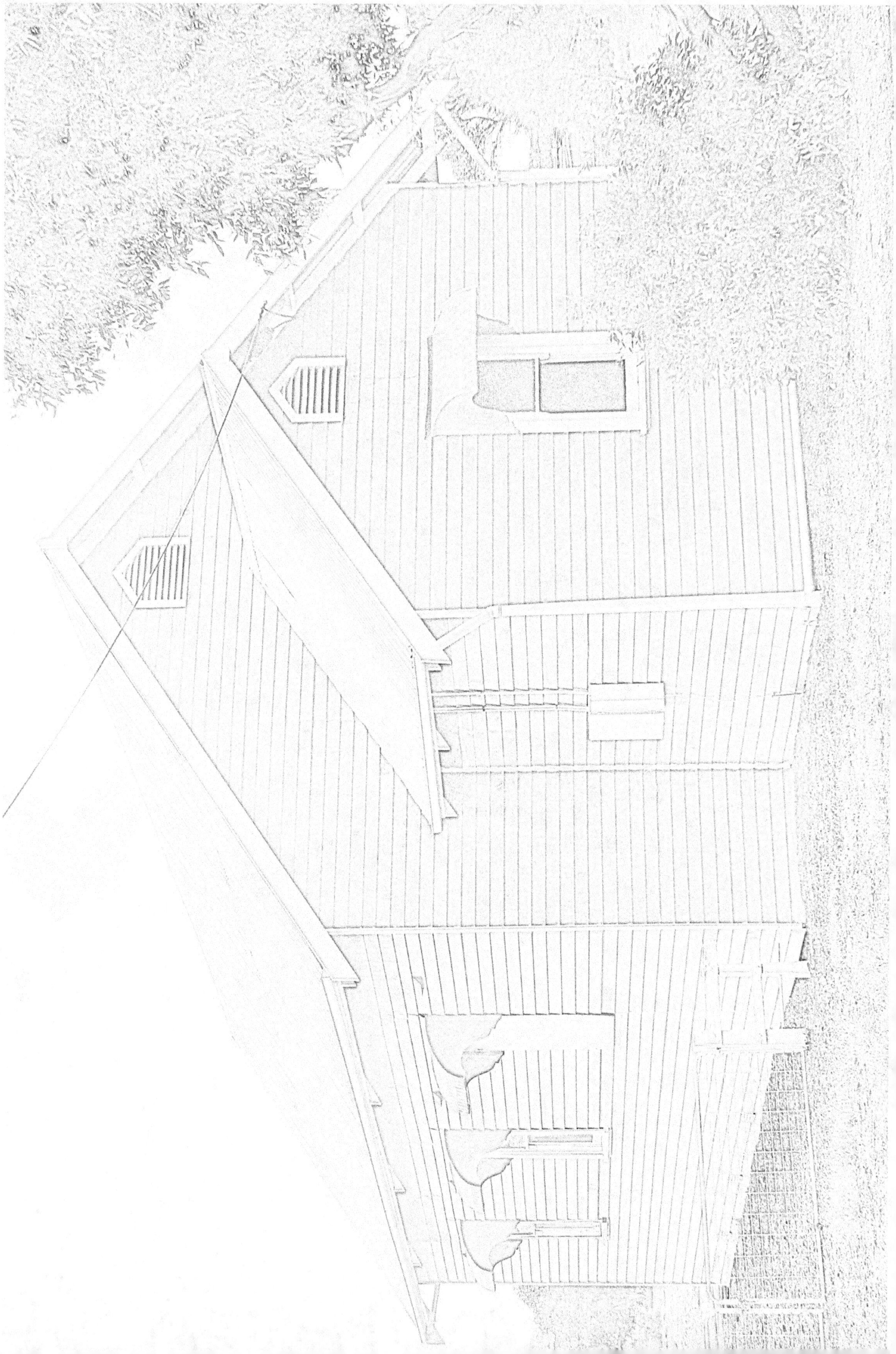

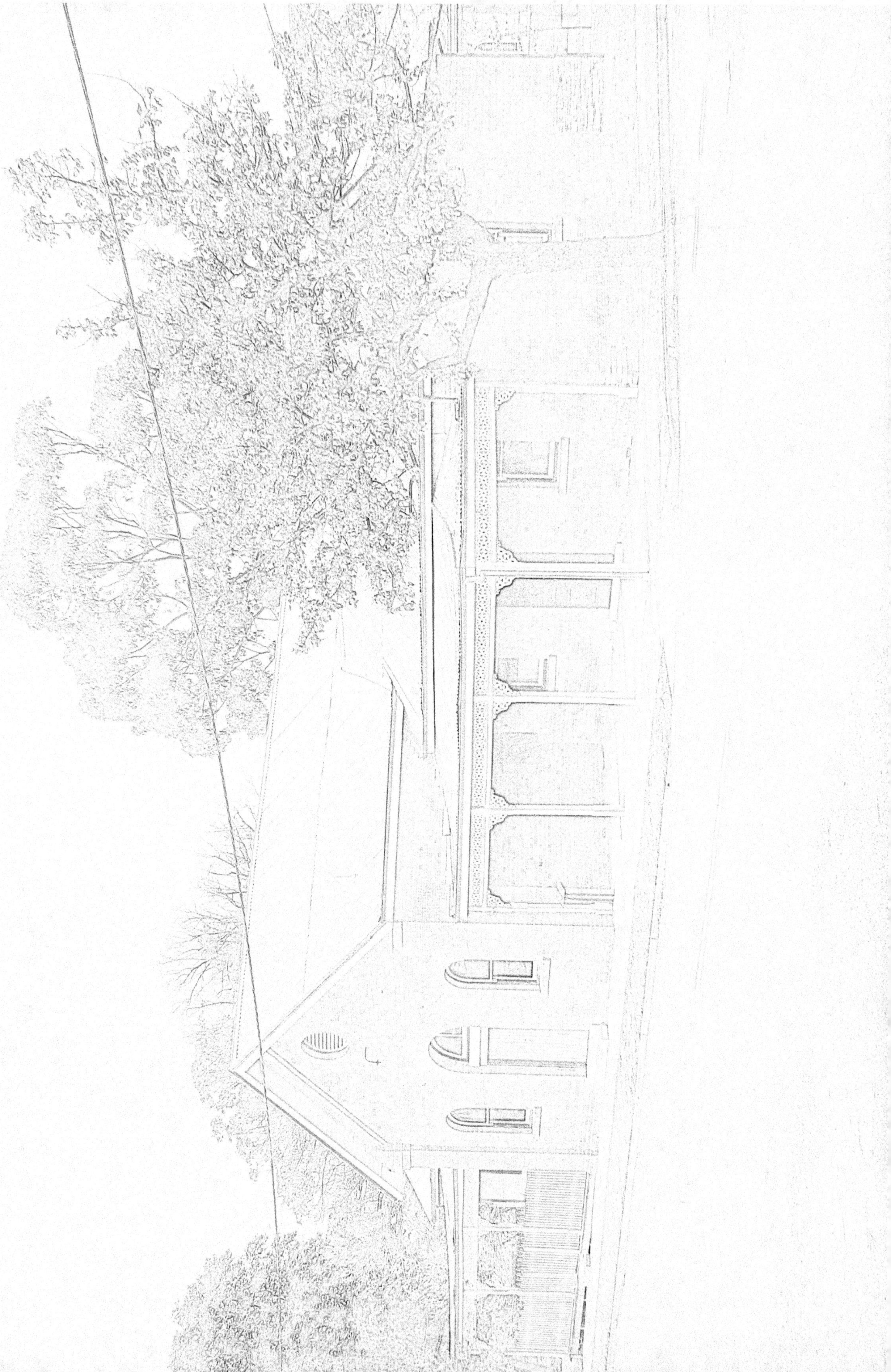

CROWN LANDS OFFICE

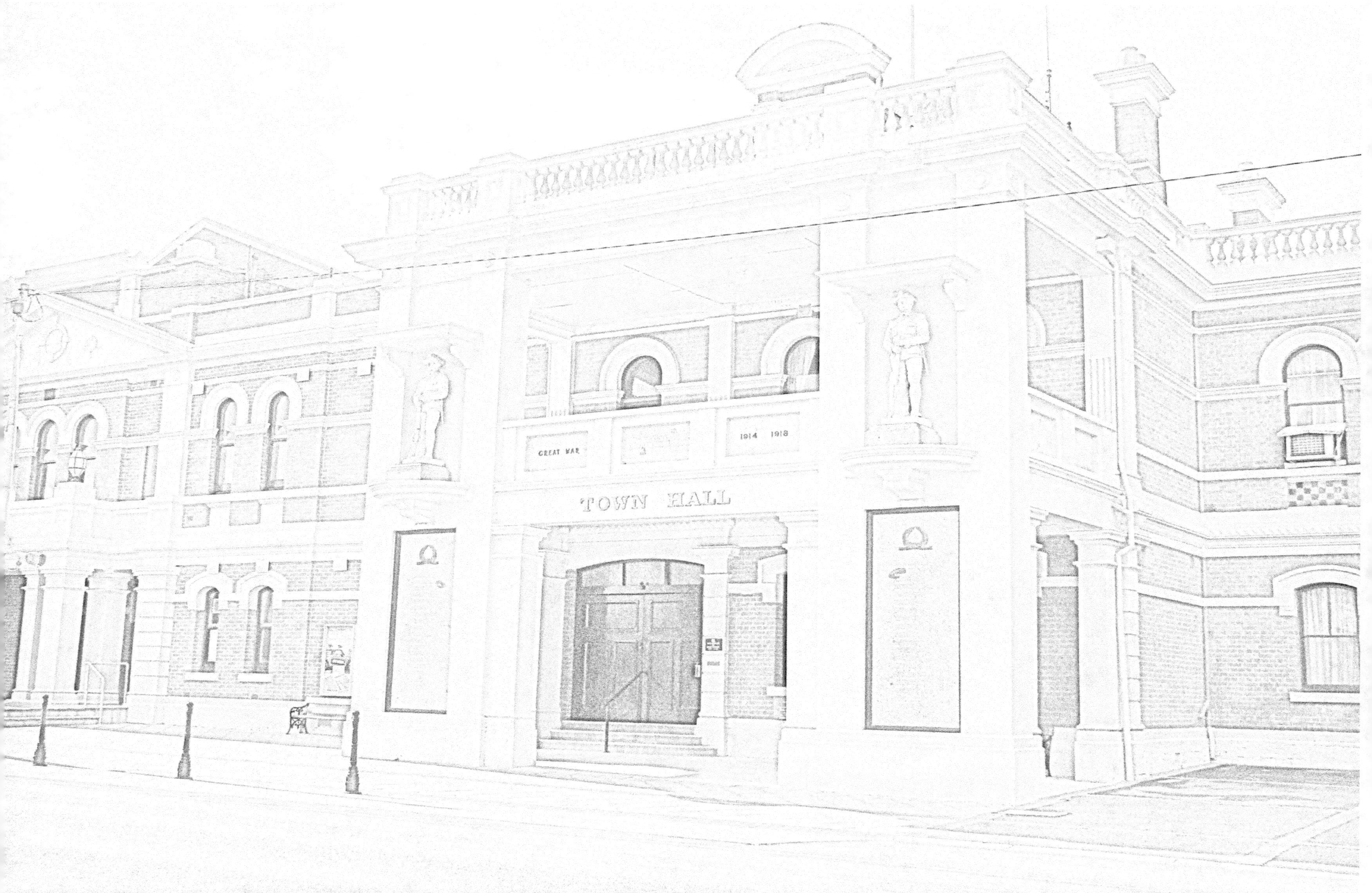
GREAT WAR
1914 1918
TOWN HALL

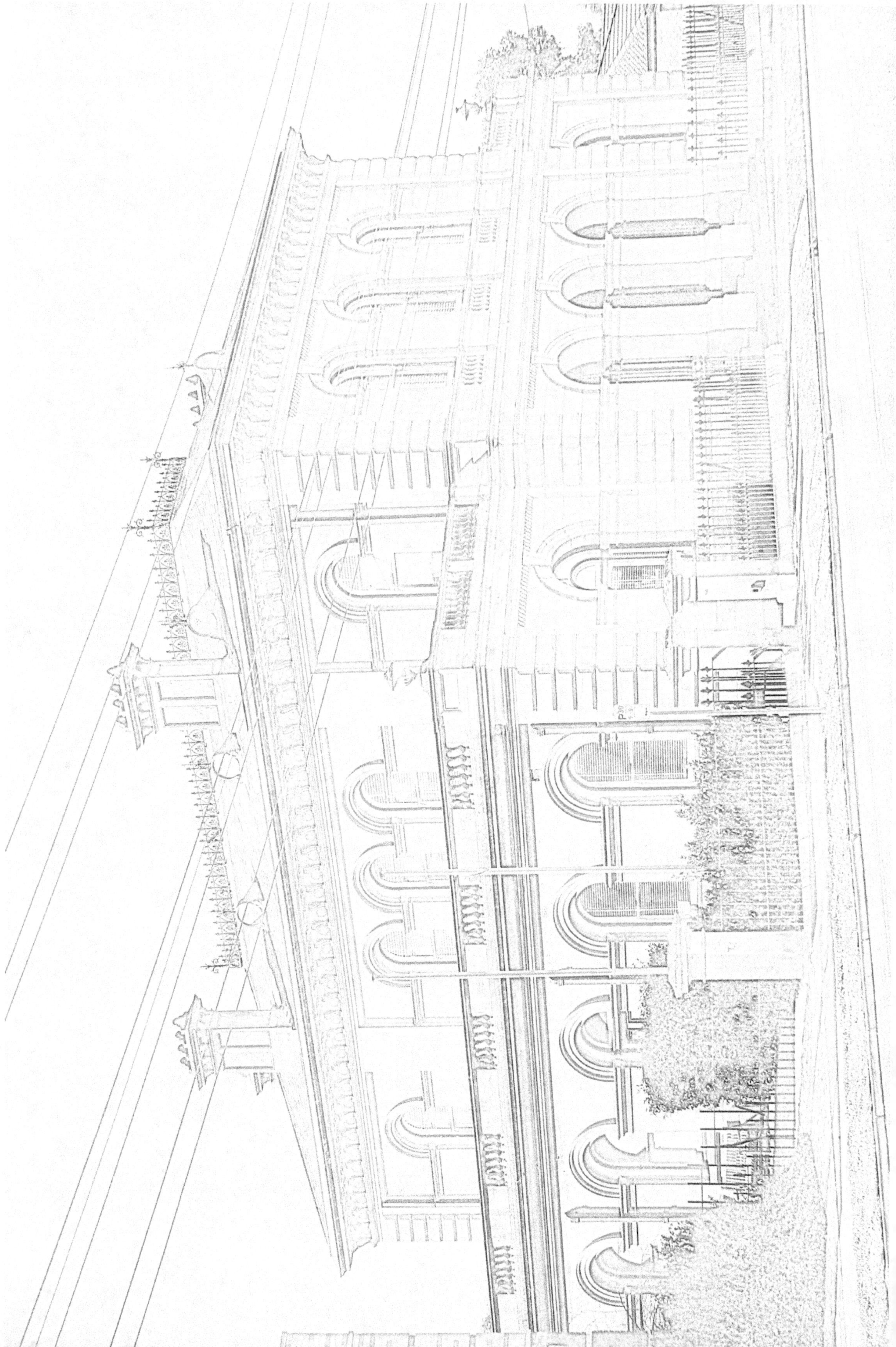

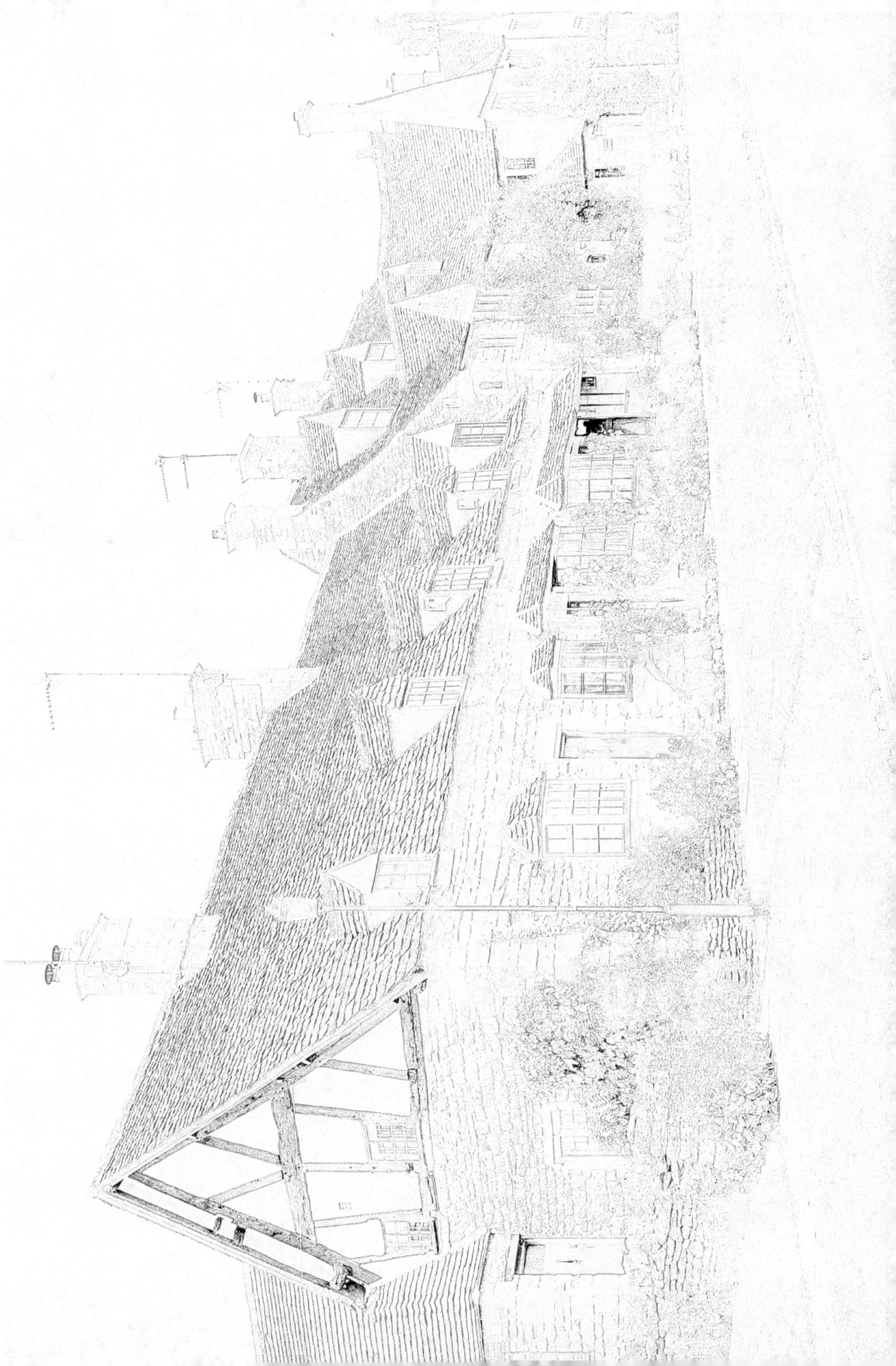

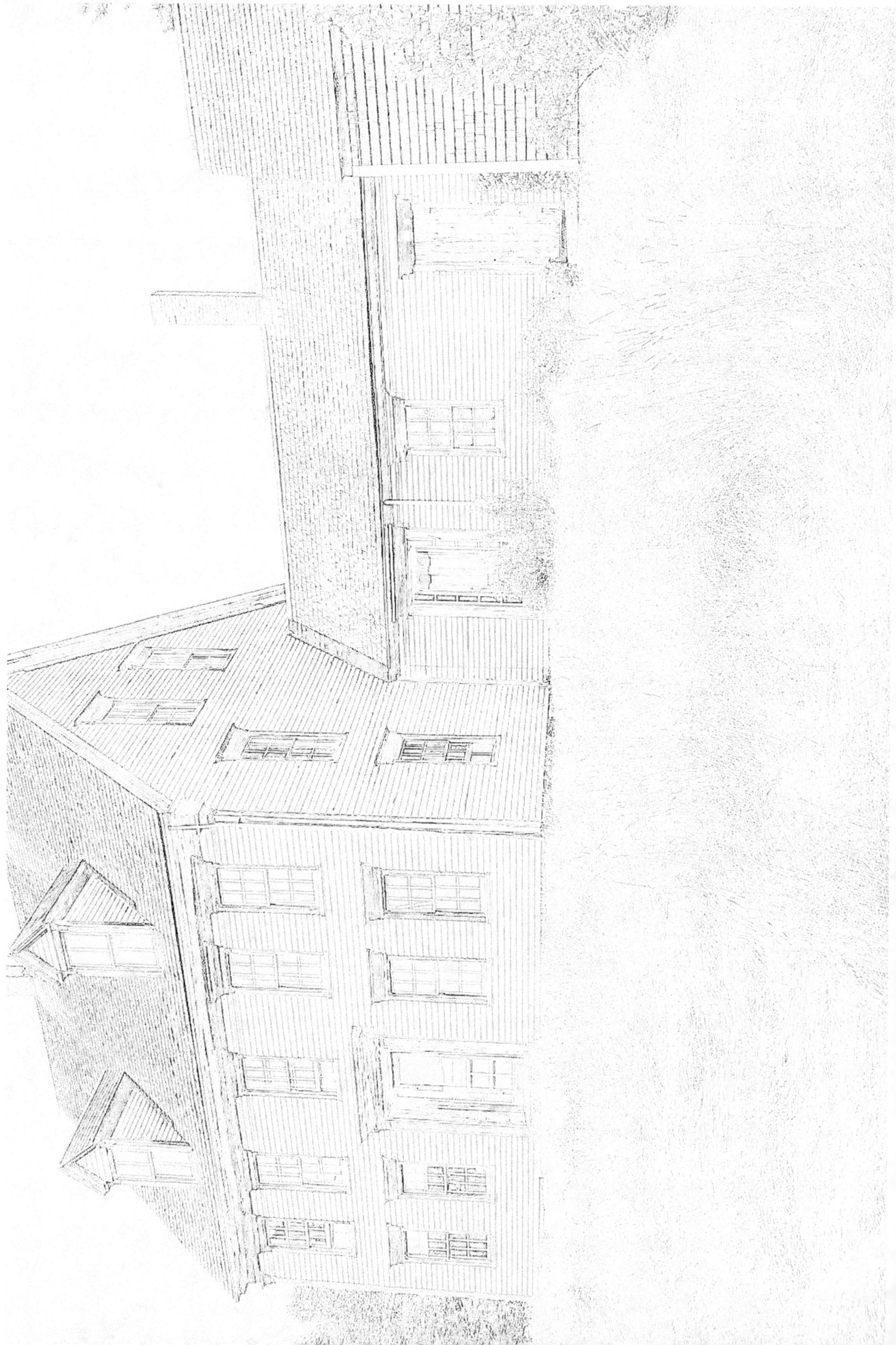

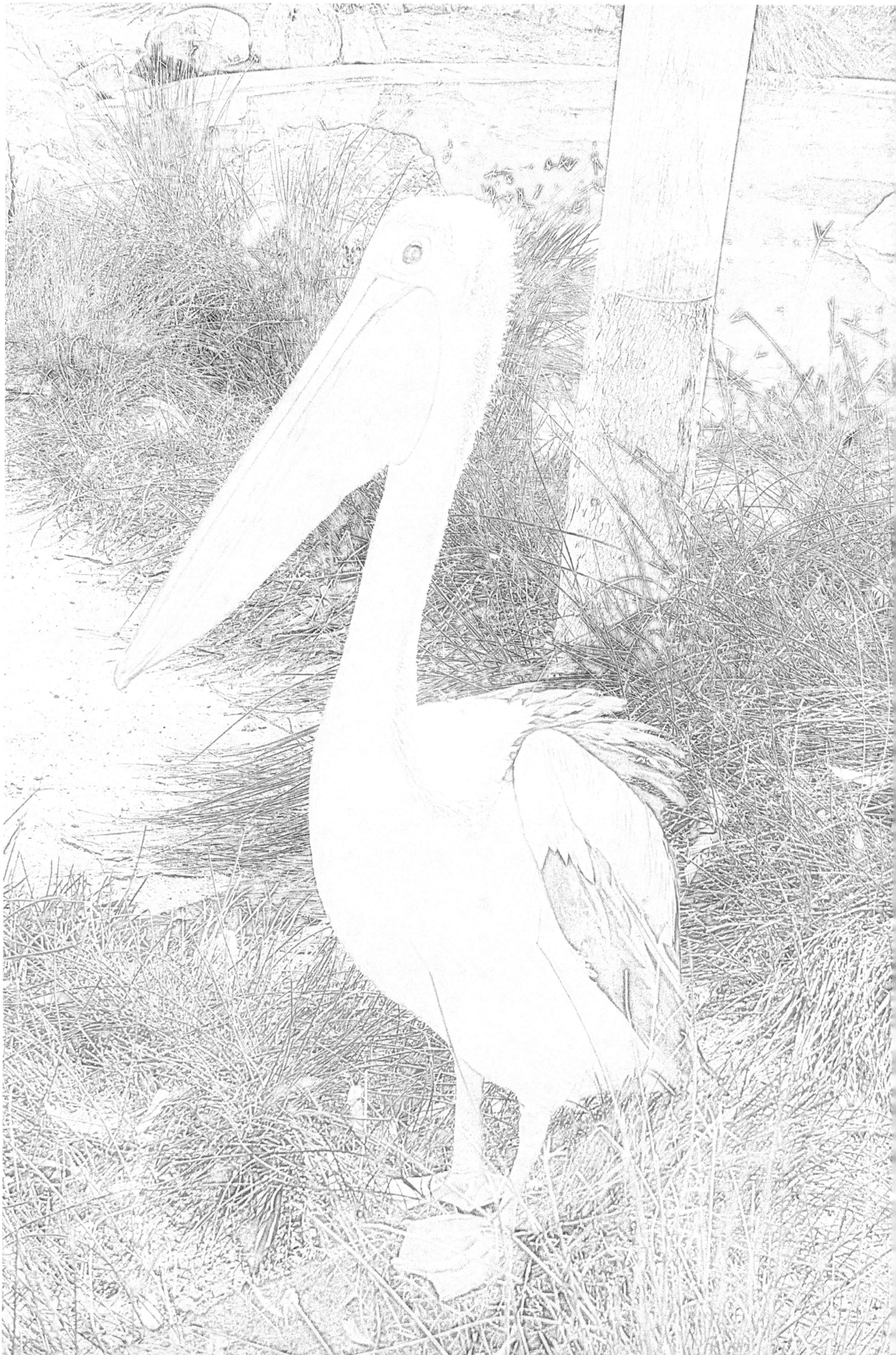

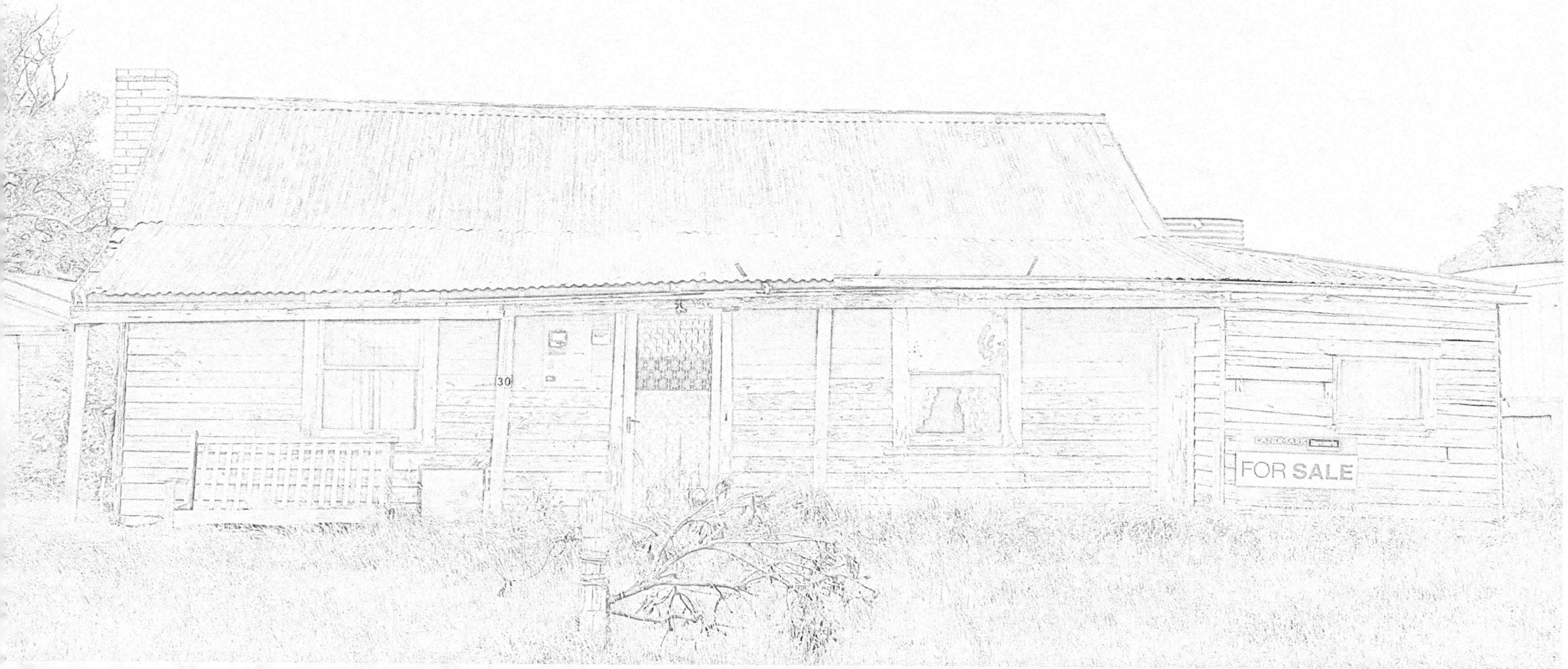
30
FOR SALE

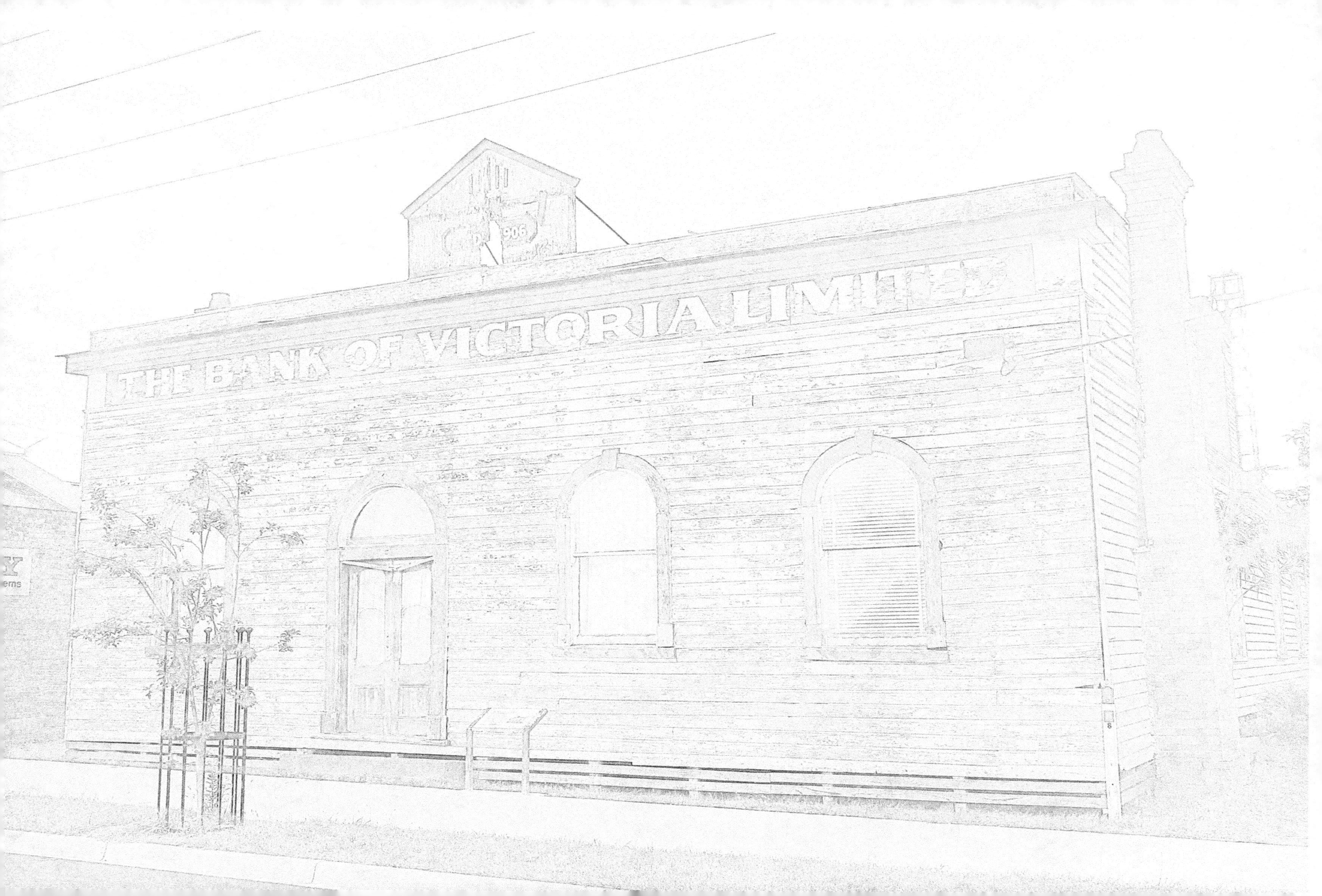
THE BANK OF VICTORIA LIMITED
1906

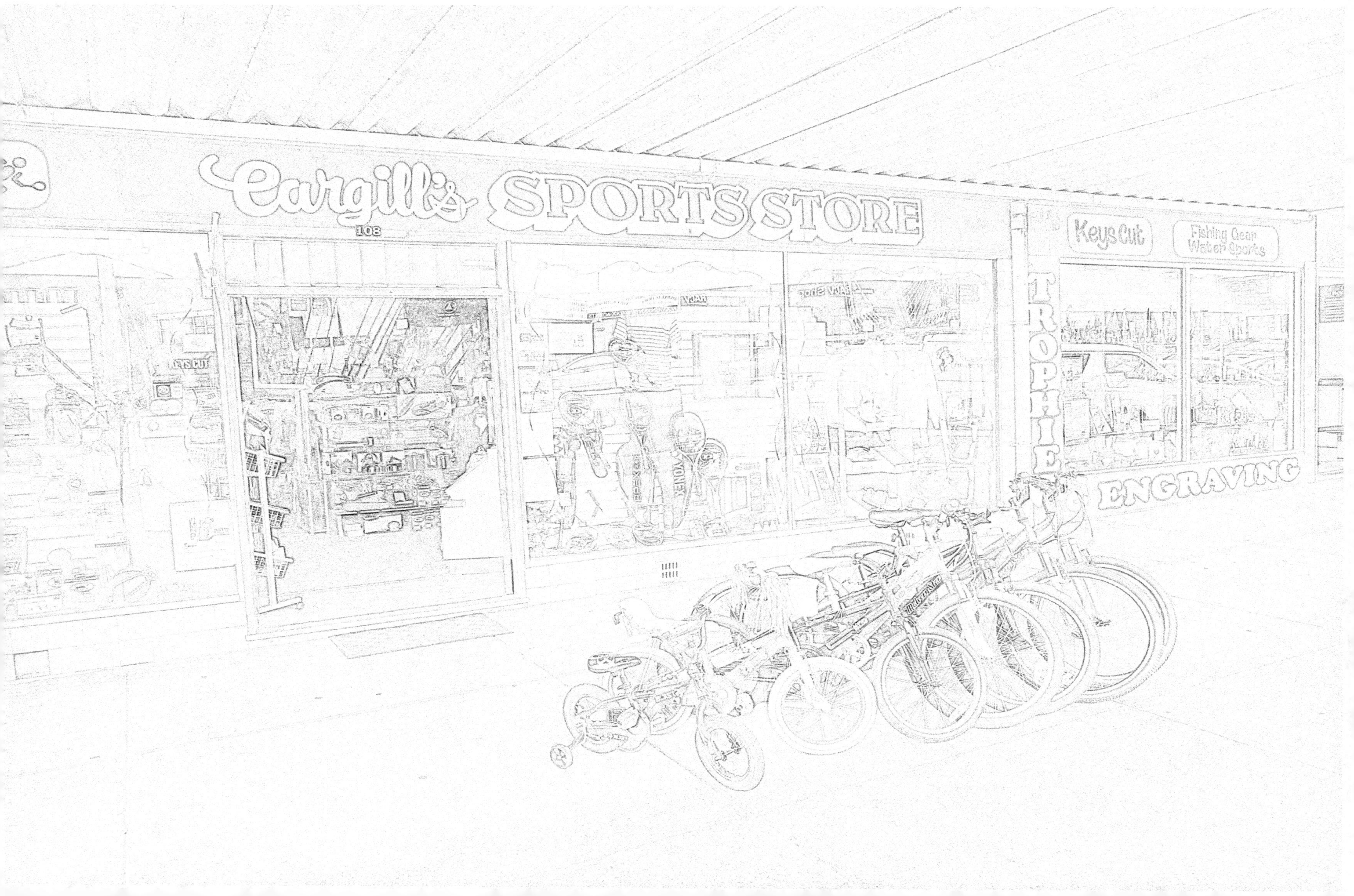

Cargill's SPORTS STORE
108
Keys Cut
Fishing Gear
Water Sports
TROPHIE
ENGRAVING
KEYS CUT
YONEX

PALAIS THEATRE
Welcome to the Palais Theatre

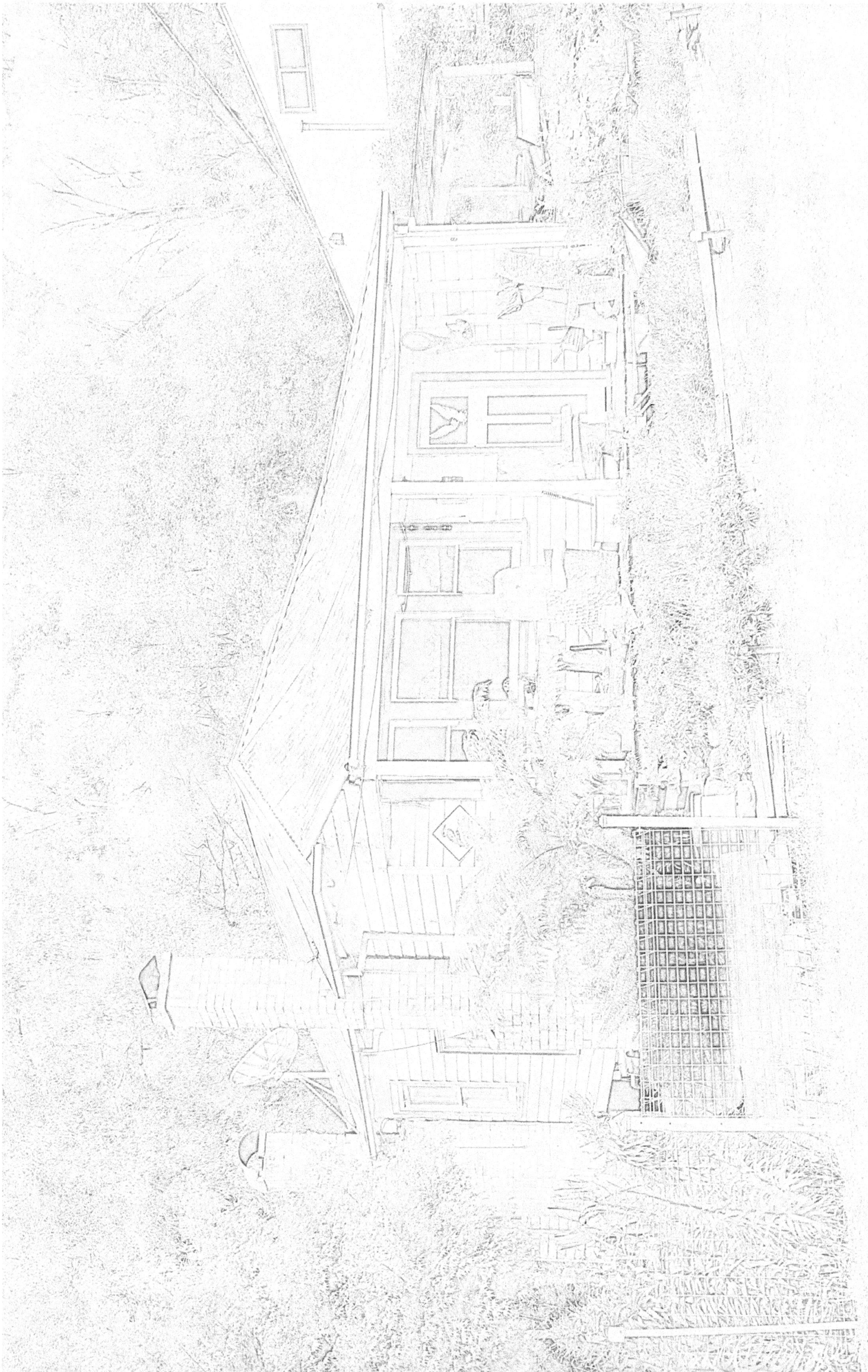

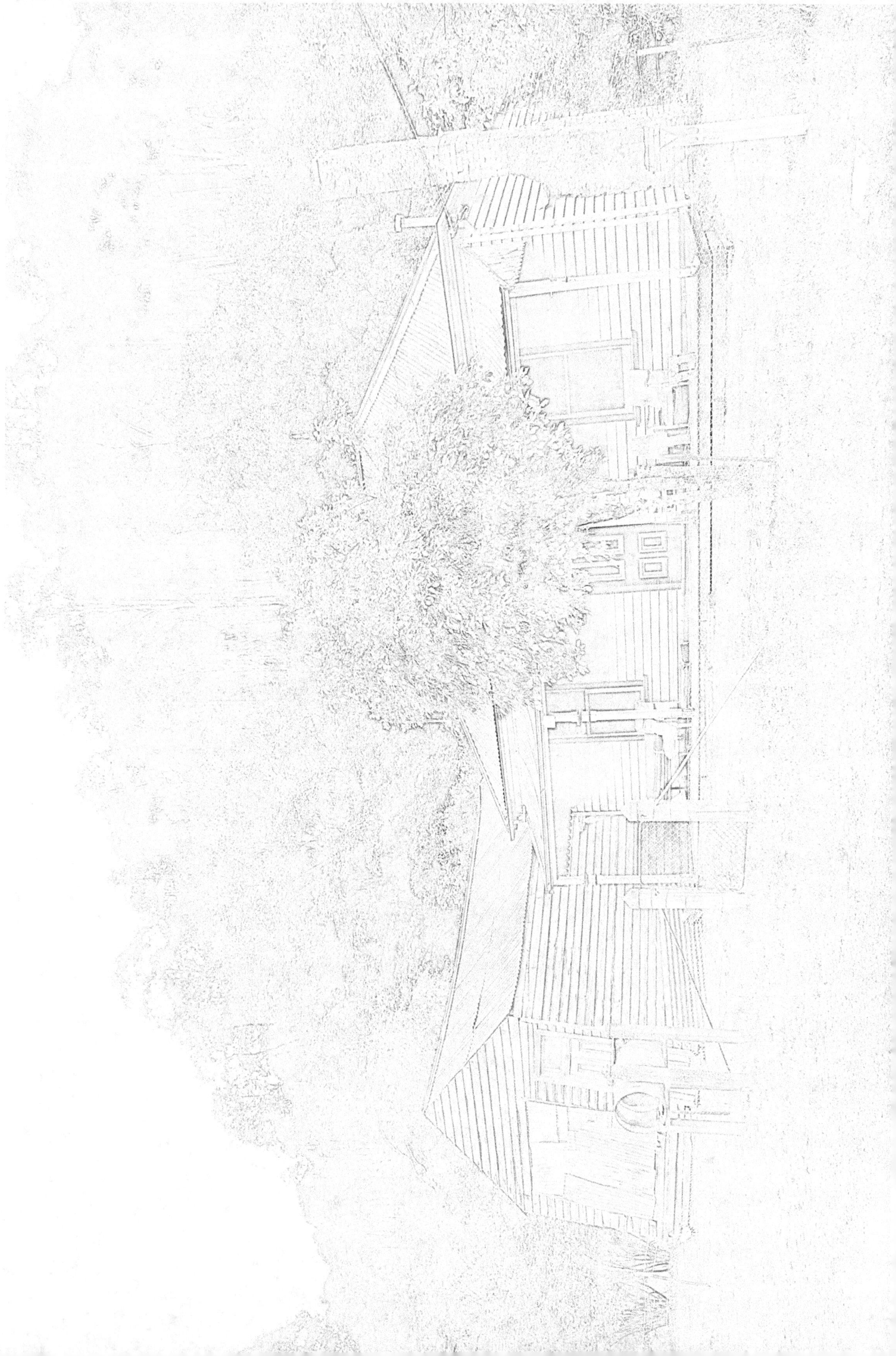

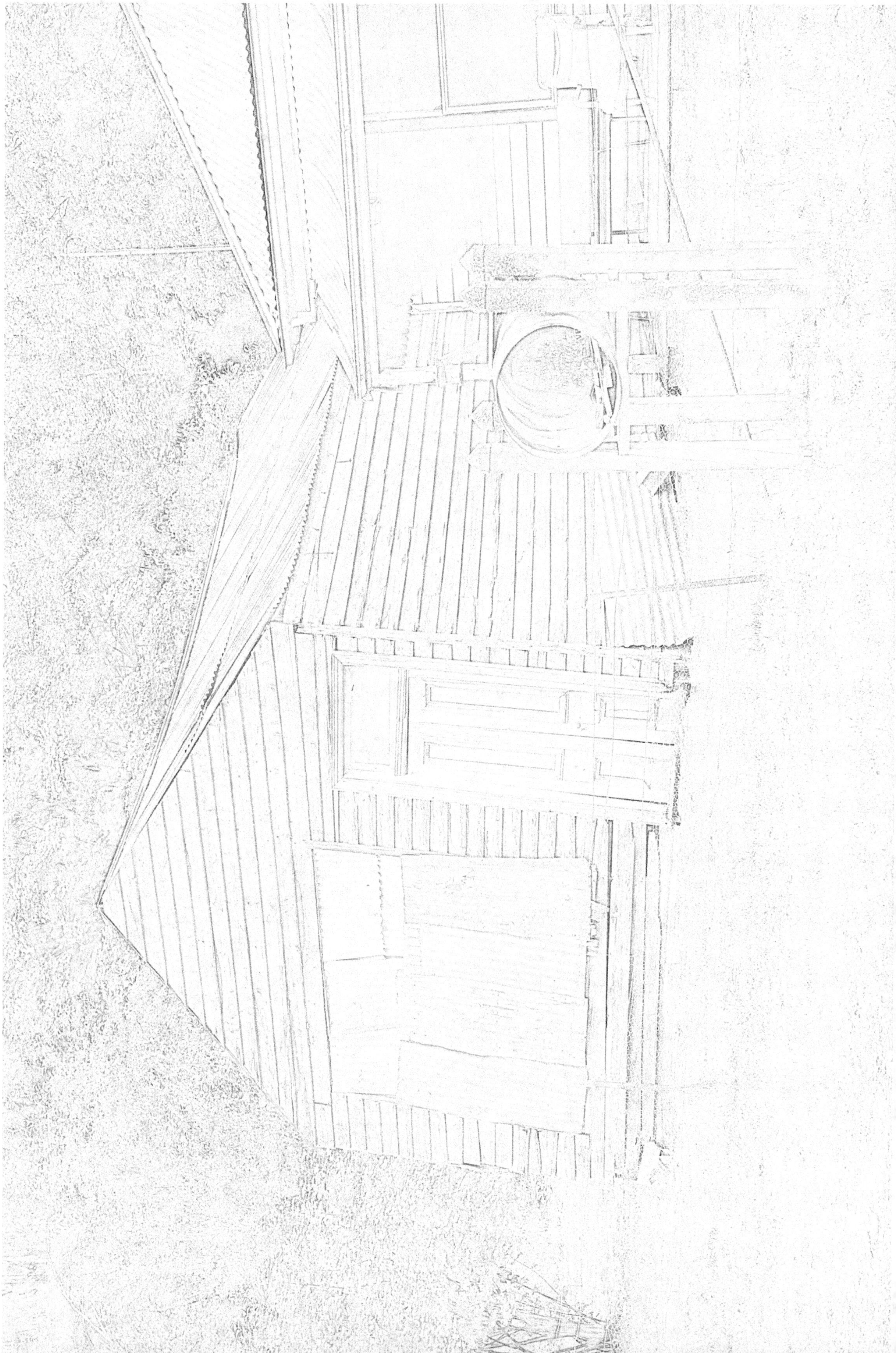

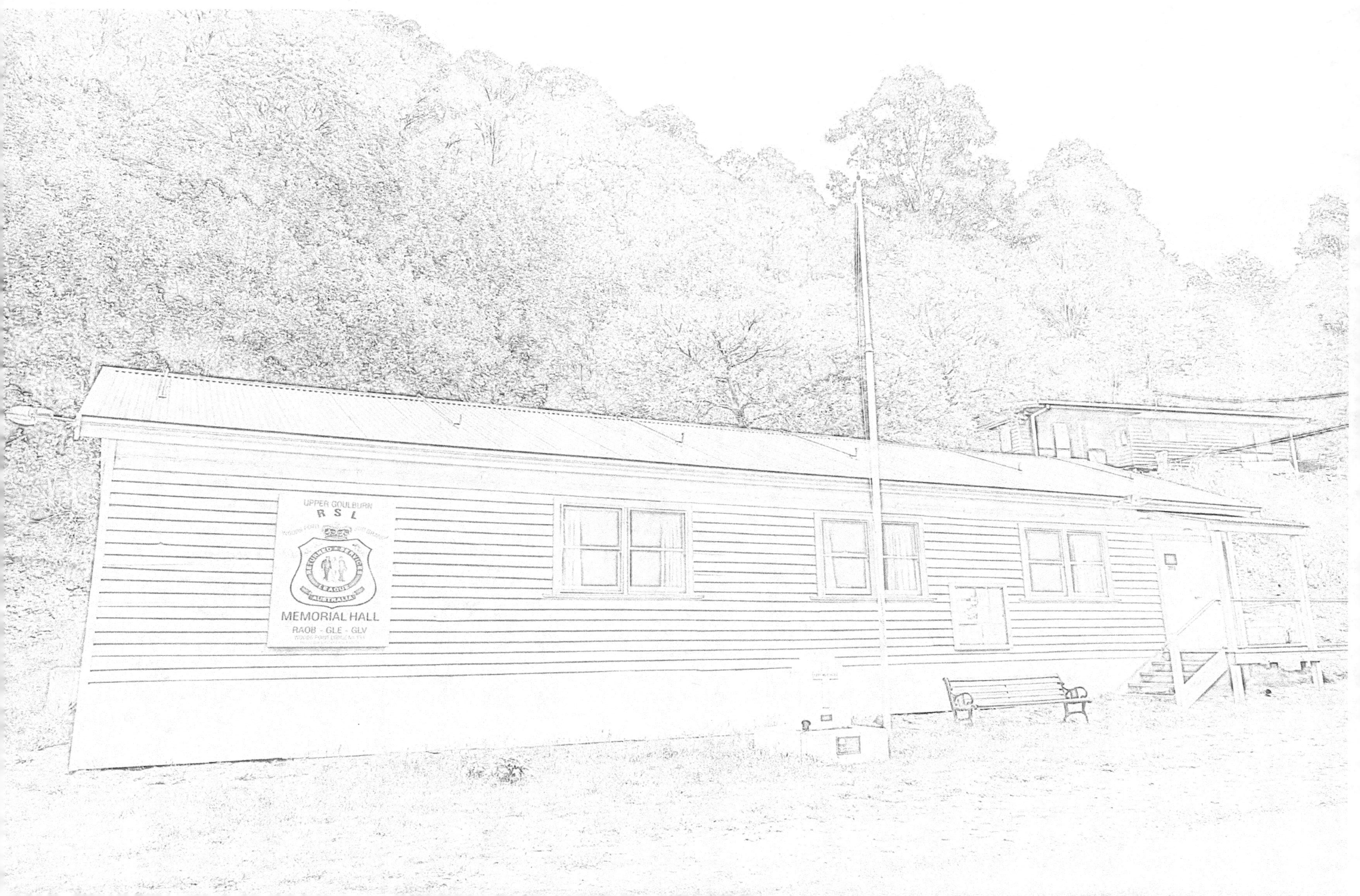
UPPER GOULBURN
RSL
MEMORIAL HALL
RAOB - GLE - GLV

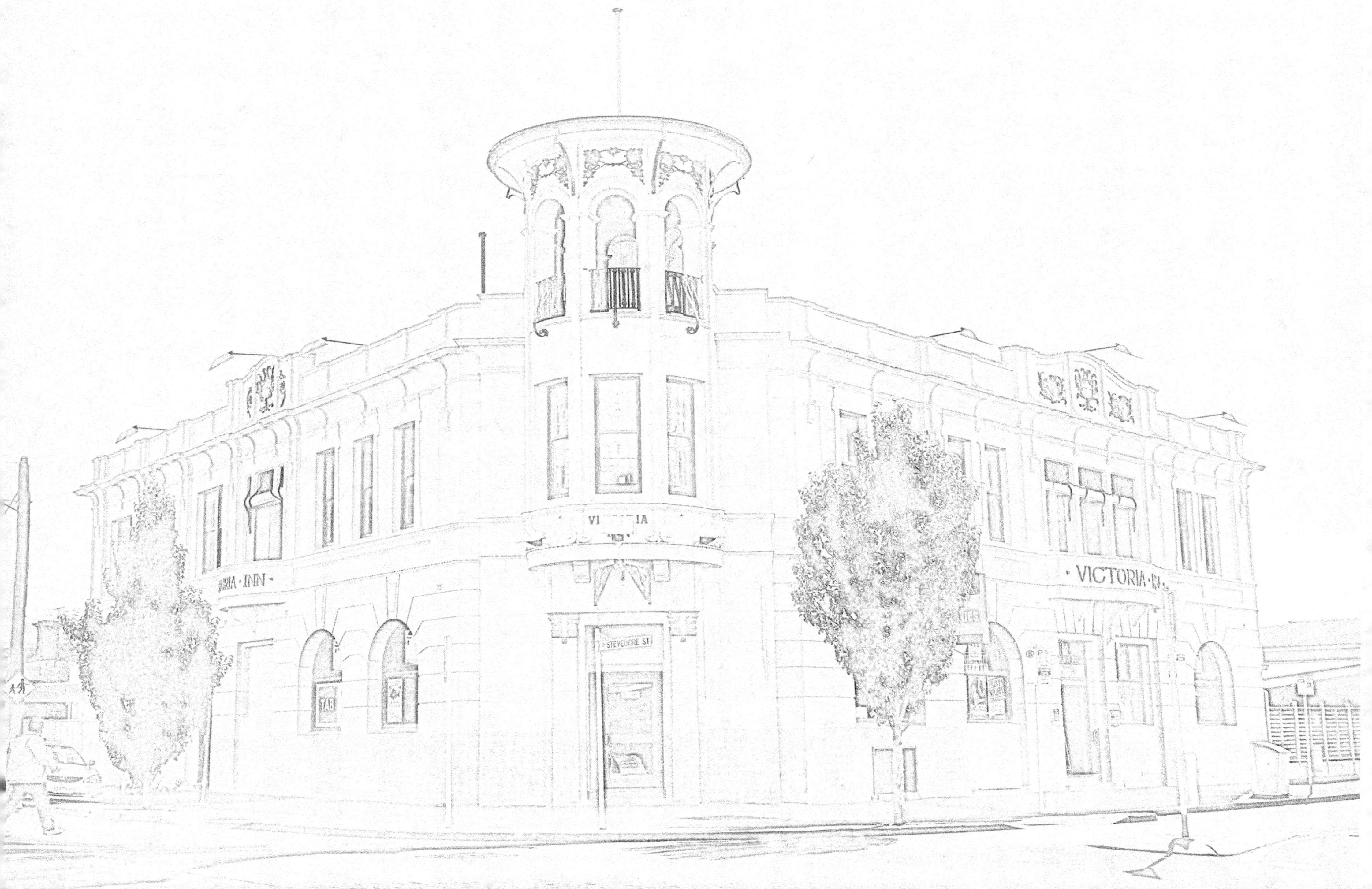

VI TIA
·RIA · INN ·
· VICTORIA ·
STEVEDORE ST
TAB

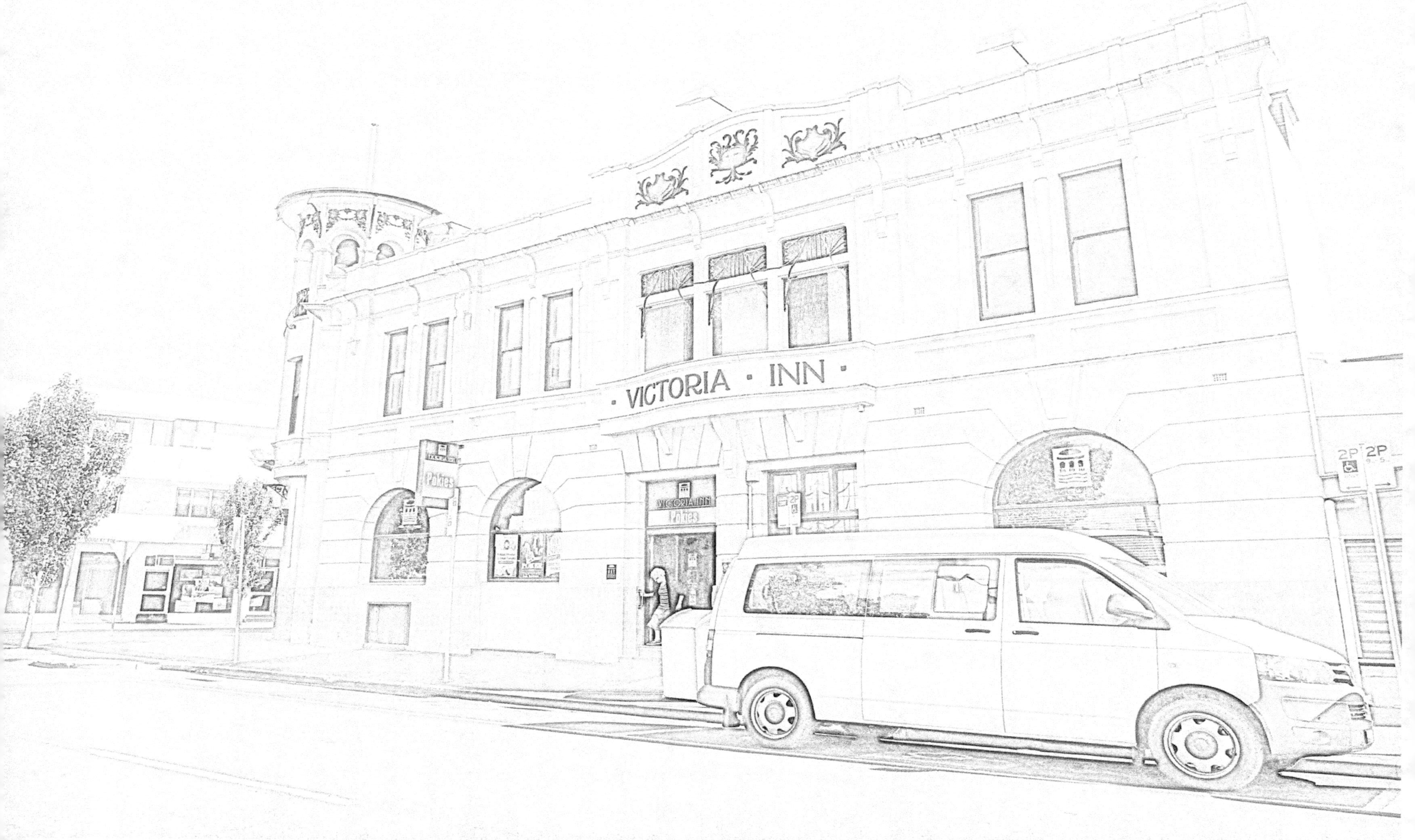

· VICTORIA · INN ·
VICTORIA INN
Pokies
Pokies
2P
2P

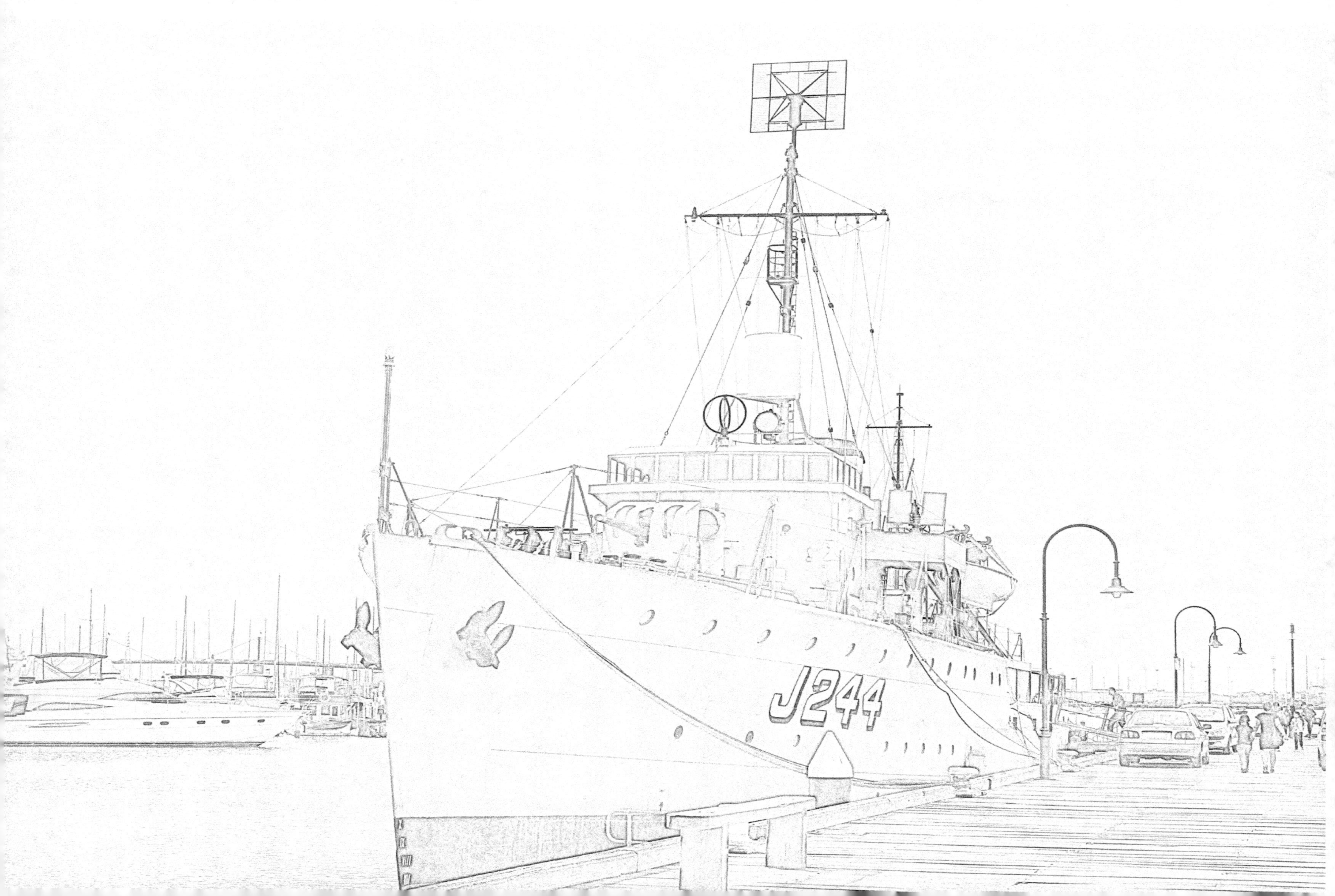
J244

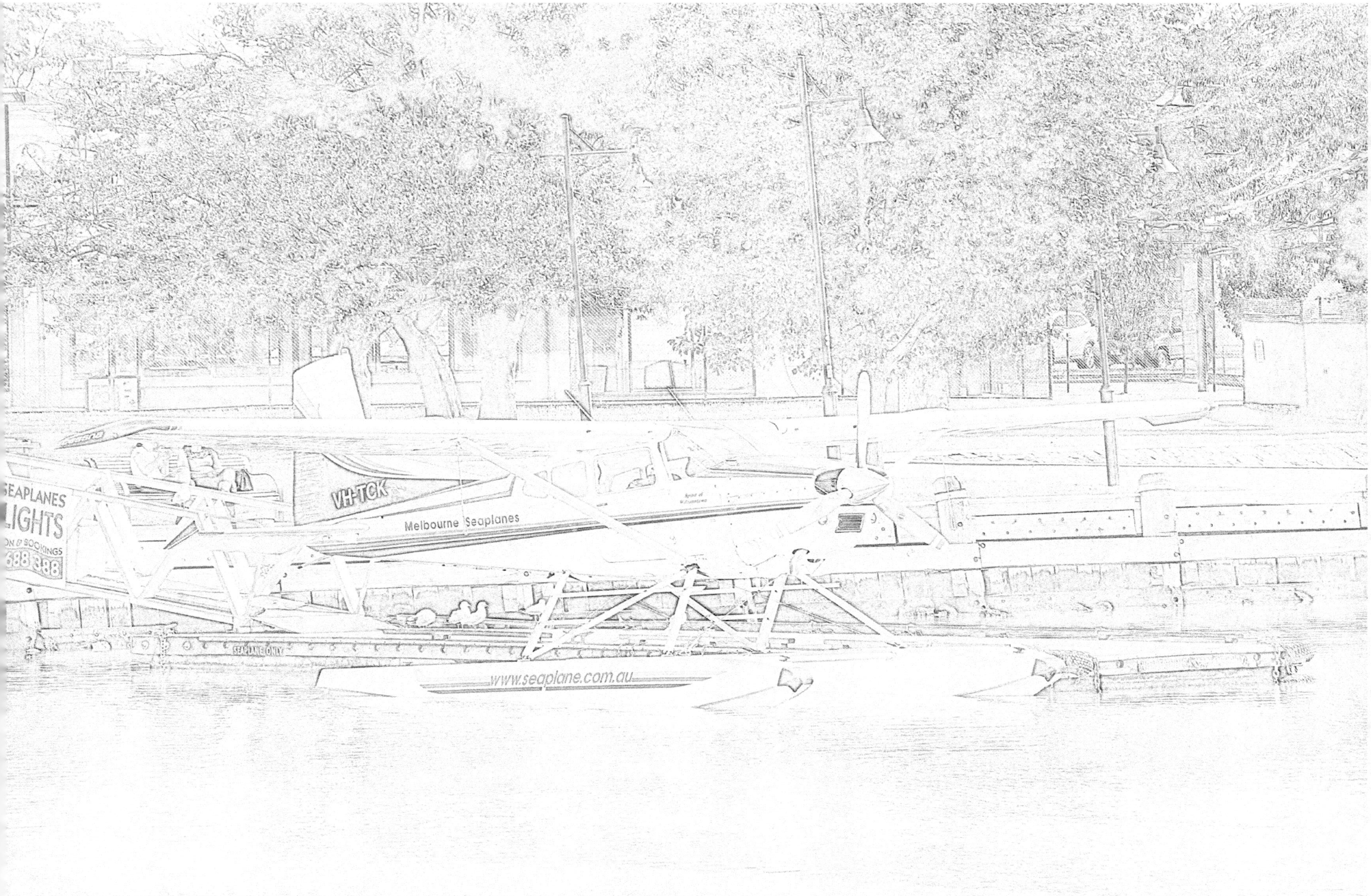
SEAPLANES
LIGHTS
VH-TCK
Melbourne Seaplanes
SEAPLANE ONLY
www.seaplane.com.au

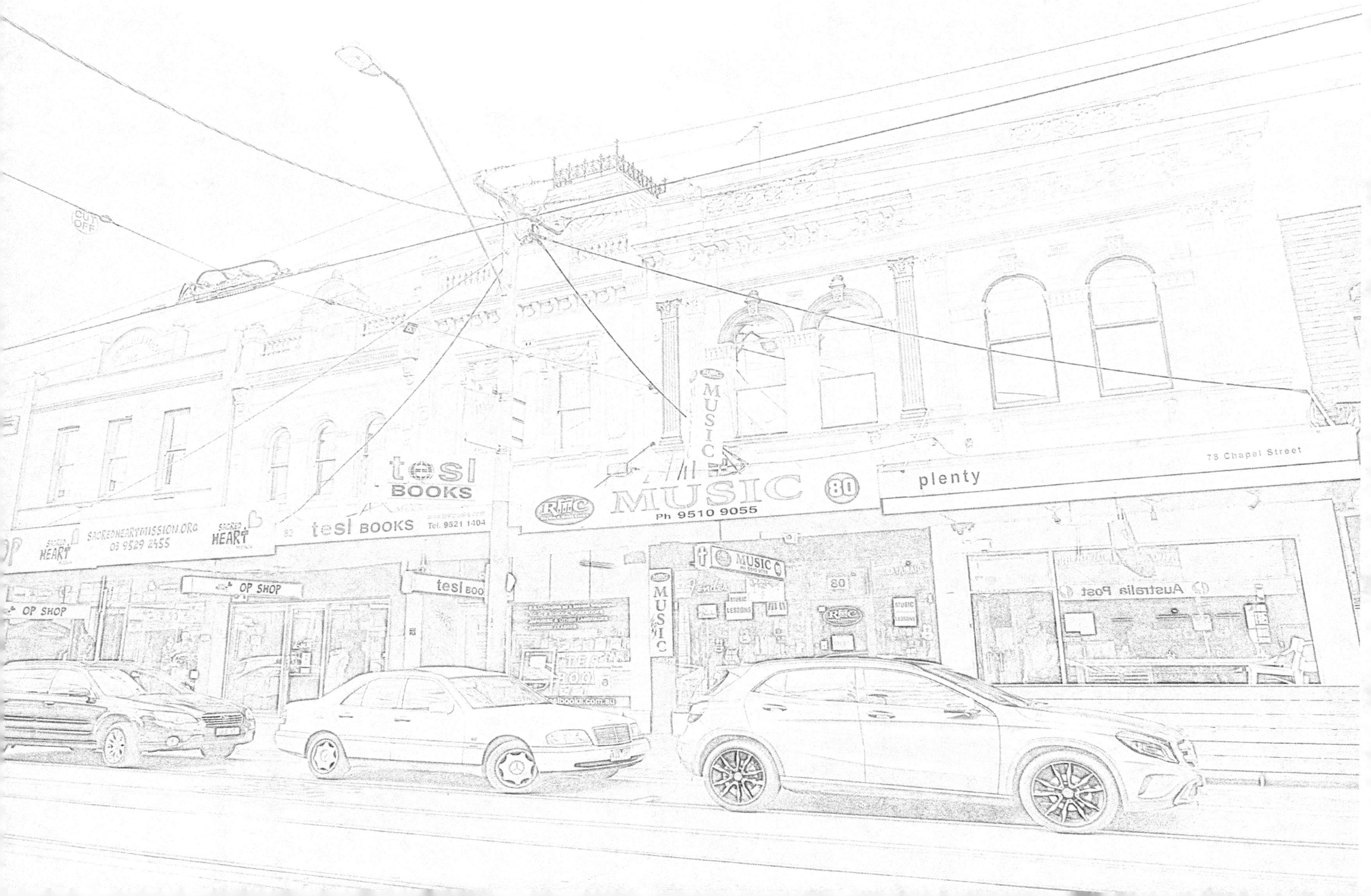
CUT OFF
SACRED HEART
SACREDHEARTMISSION.ORG
03 9529 2455
SACRED HEART
OP SHOP
OP SHOP
tesl BOOKS
tesl BOOKS Tel. 9521 1404
tesl BOO
MUSIC
RMC MUSIC 80
Ph 9510 9055
MUSIC
MUSIC
80
MUSIC LESSONS
plenty
78 Chapel Street
Australia Post

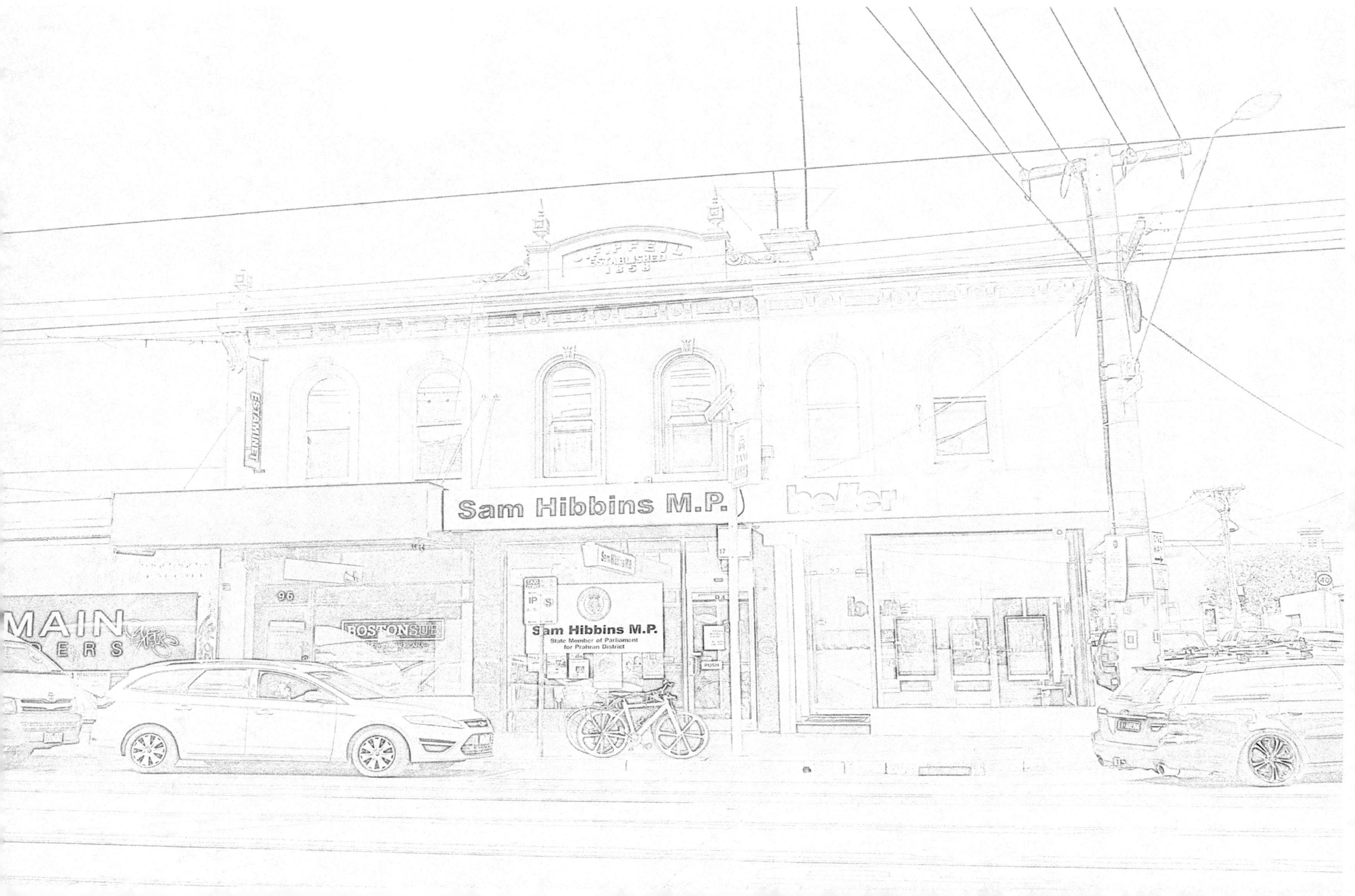
Sam Hibbins M.P.
Sam Hibbins M.P.
State Member of Parliament
for Prahran District
ESTAMINET
BOSTON SUB
96
MAIN
PUSH
40

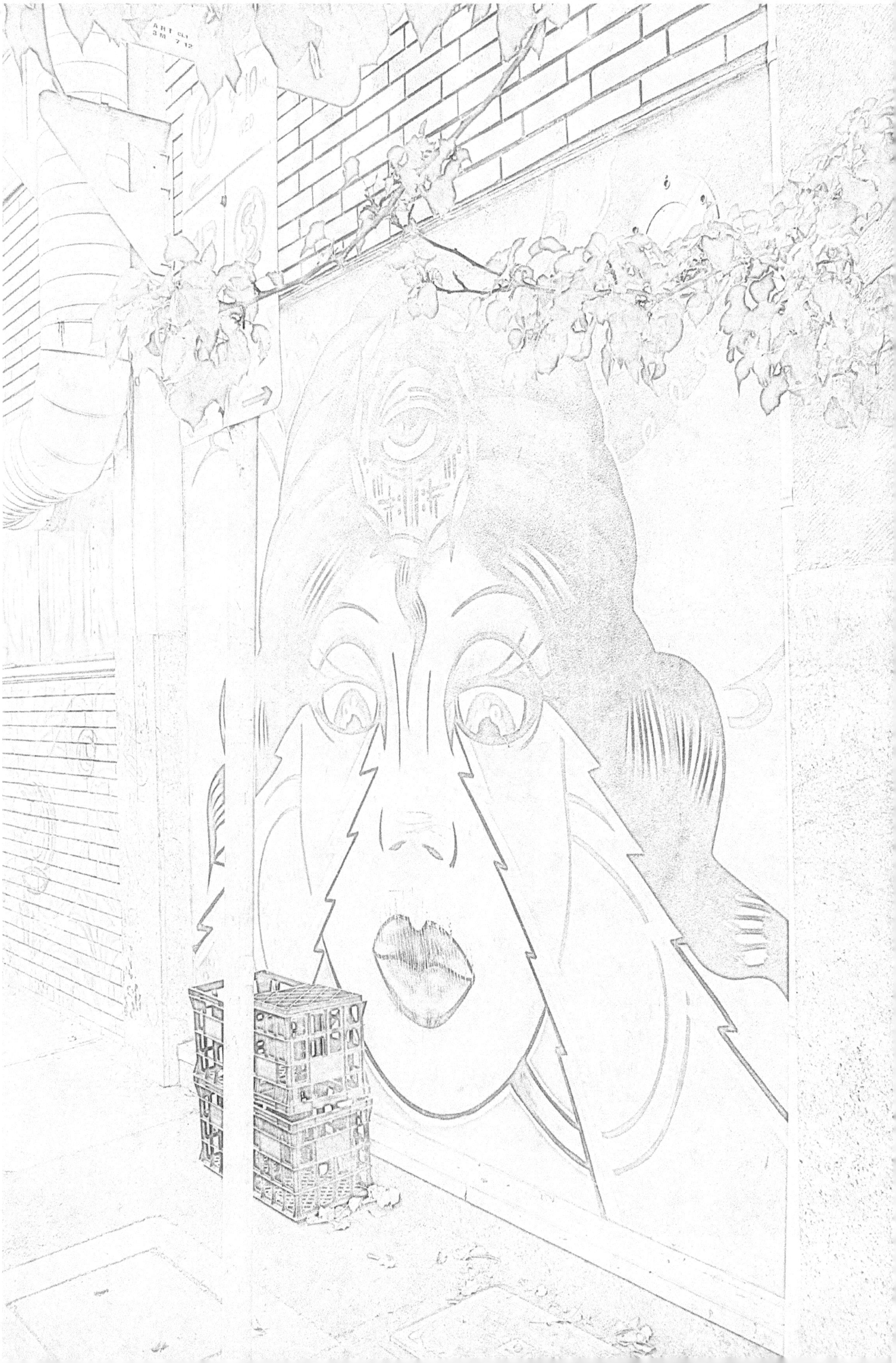

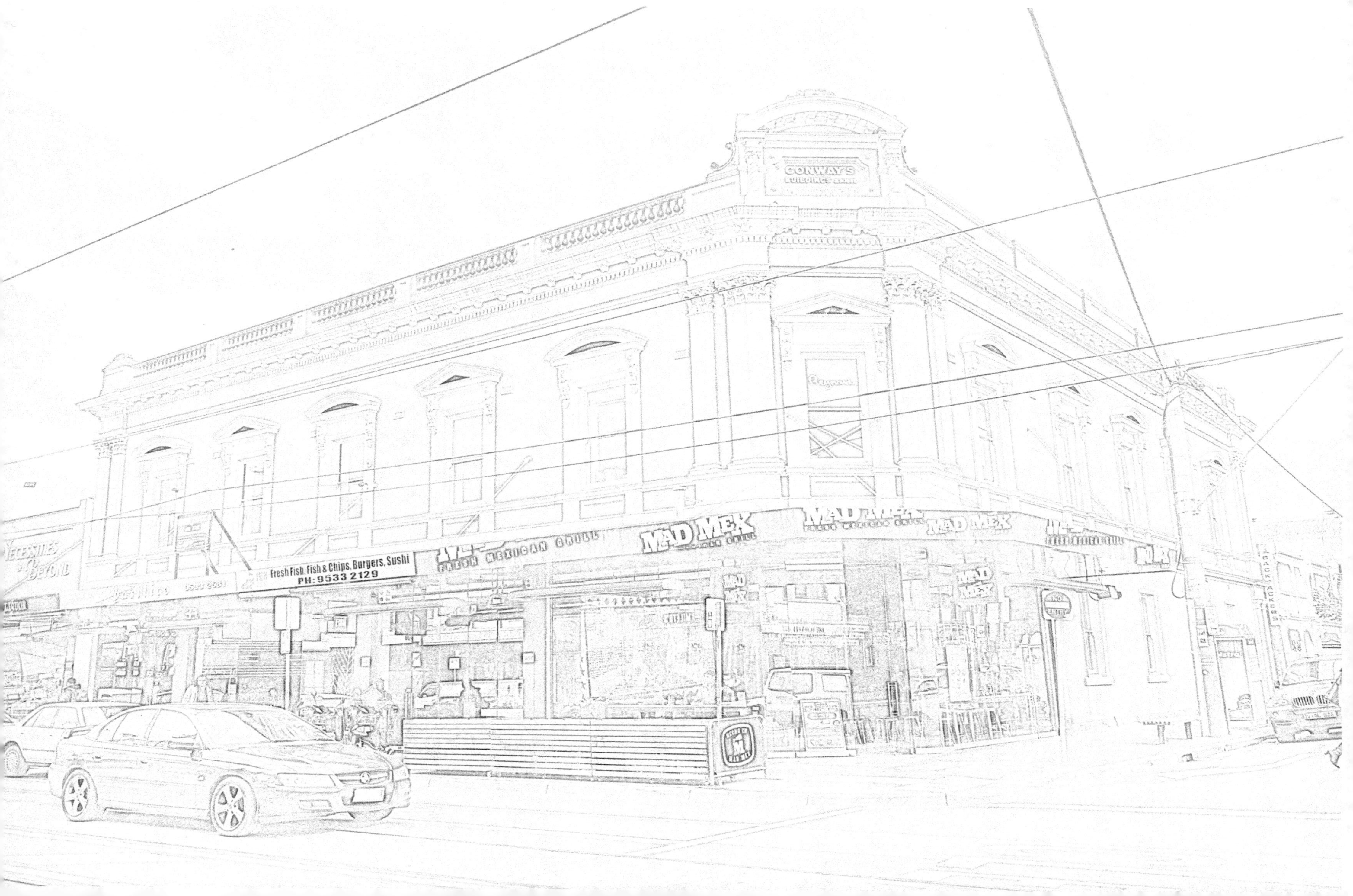
CONWAY'S
MAD MEX
FRESH MEXICAN GRILL
Fresh Fish, Fish & Chips, Burgers, Sushi
PH: 9533 2129
Necessities & Beyond

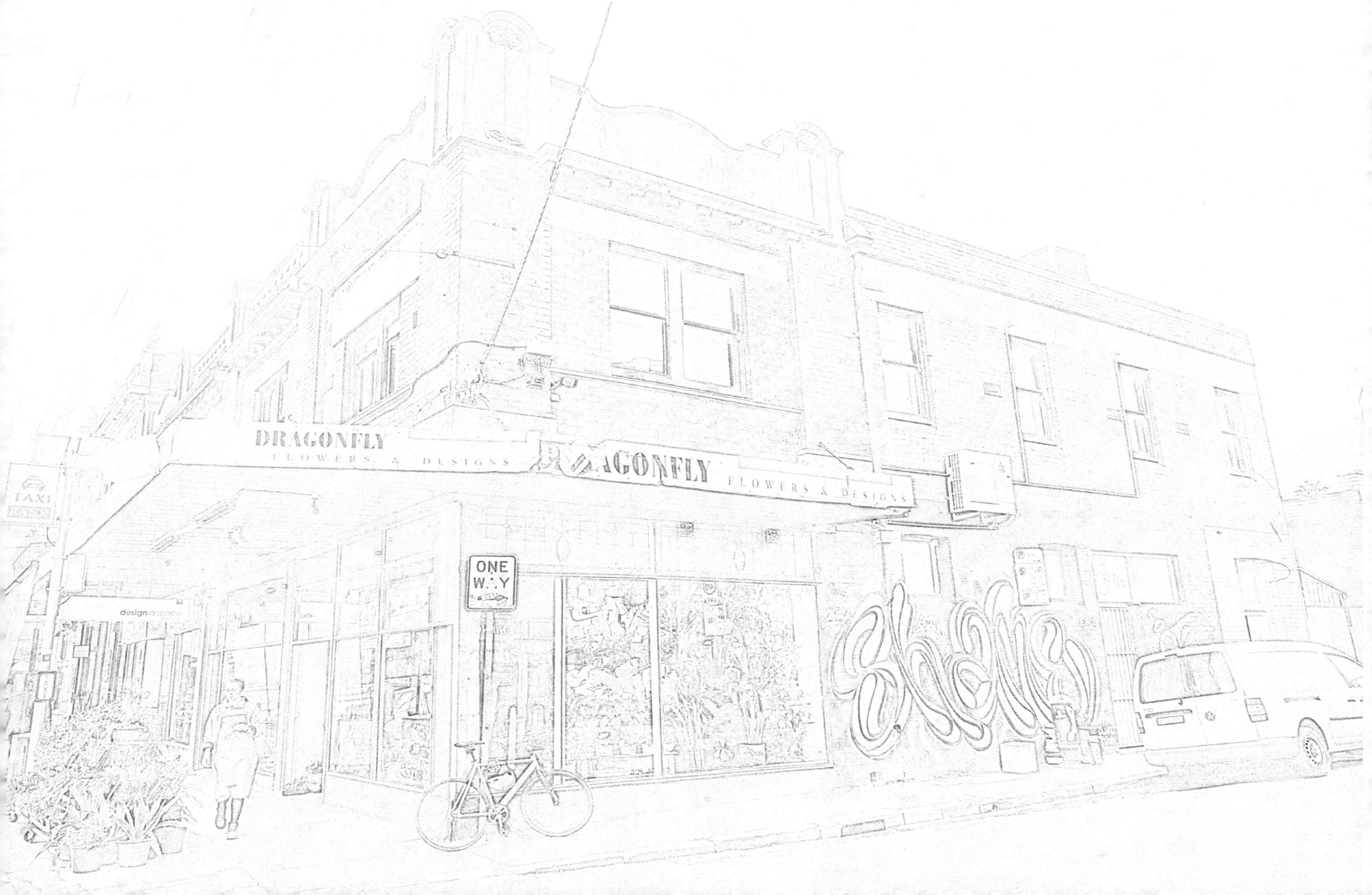
DRAGONFLY
FLOWERS & DESIGNS
DRAGONFLY
FLOWERS & DESIGNS
ONE WAY
TAXI
design a space

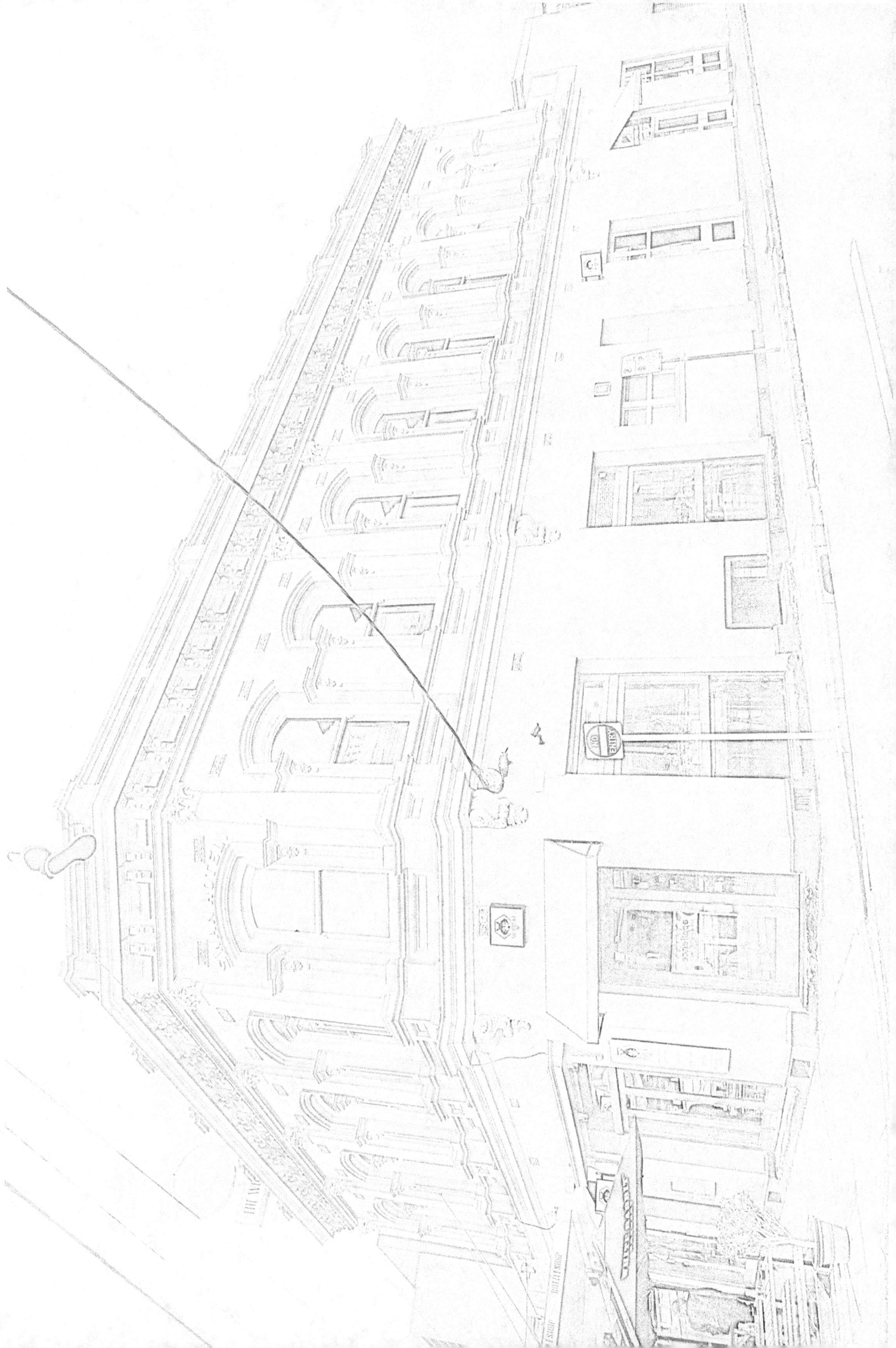

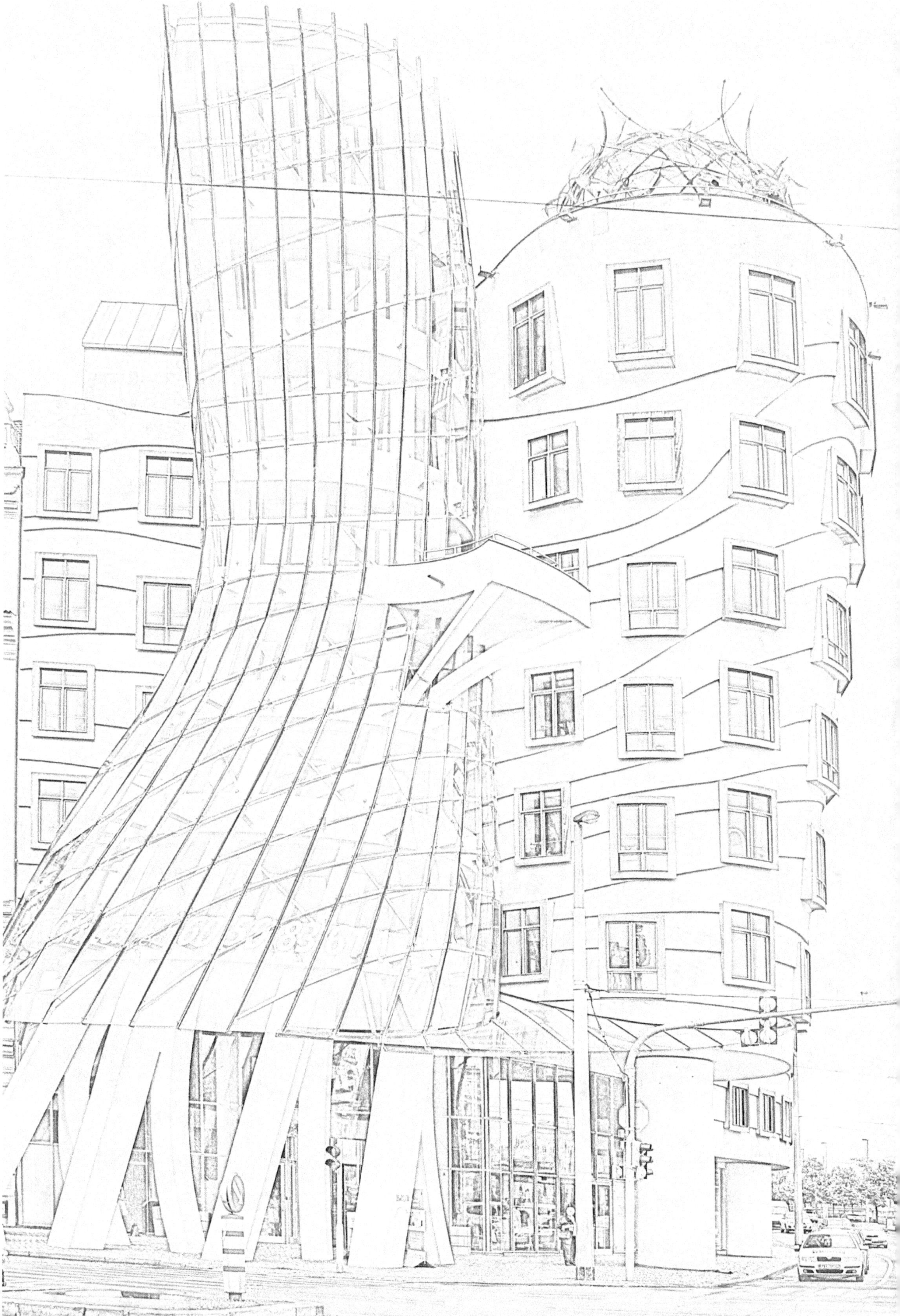

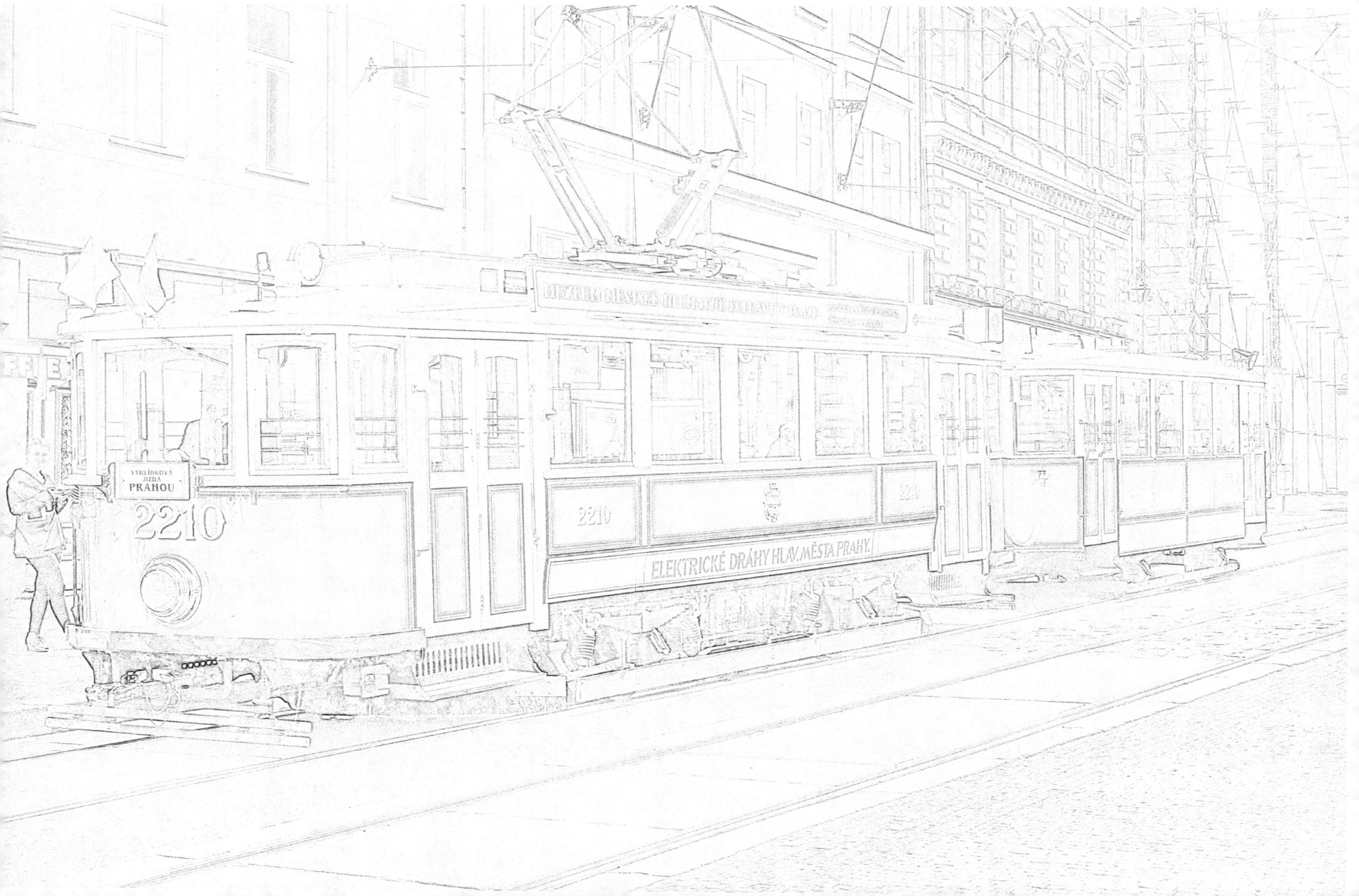
VYHLÍDKOVÁ JÍZDA PRAHOU
2210
2210
ELEKTRICKÉ DRÁHY HLAV. MĚSTA PRAHY.

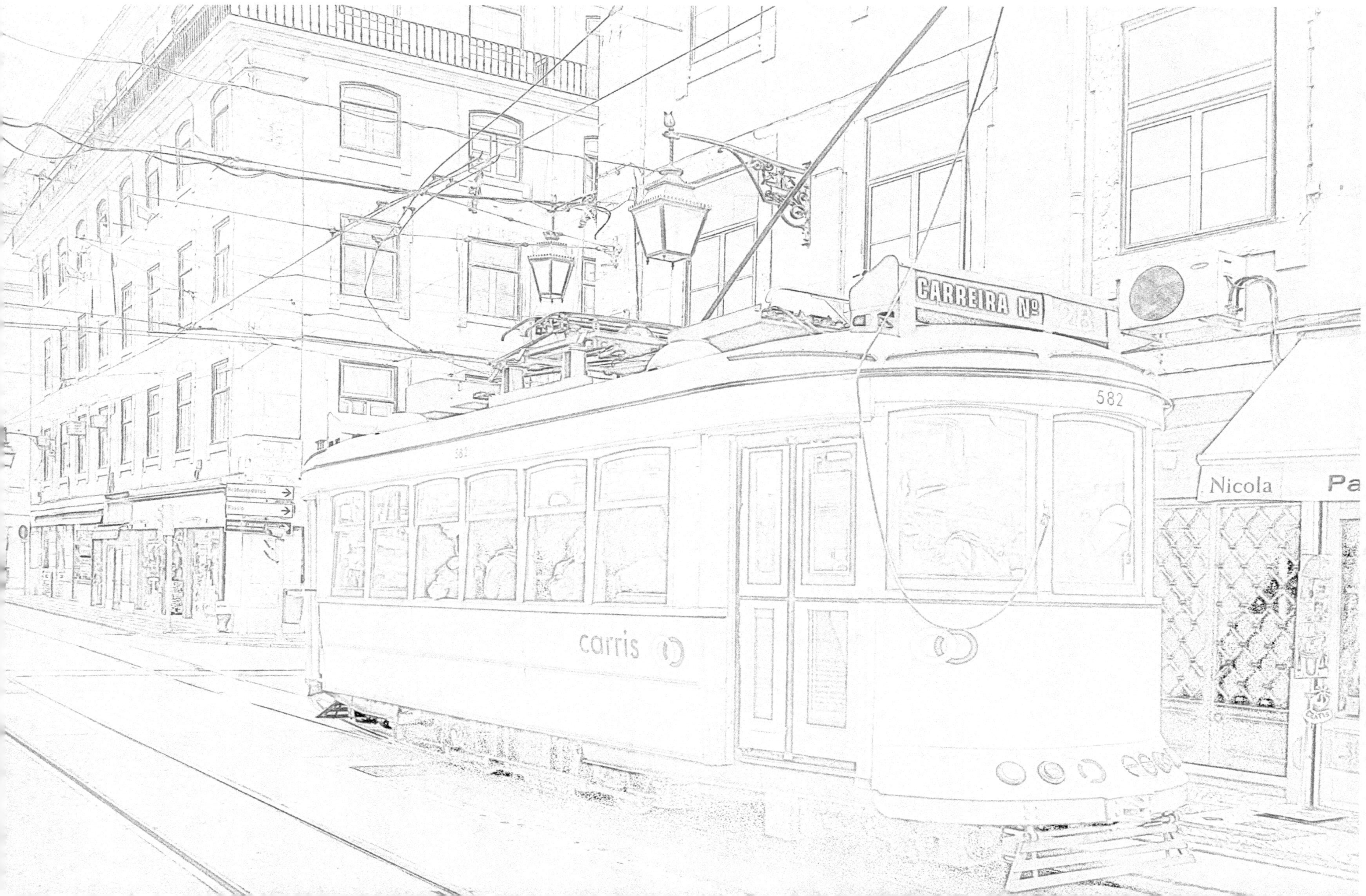
CARREIRA Nº
582
carris
Nicola

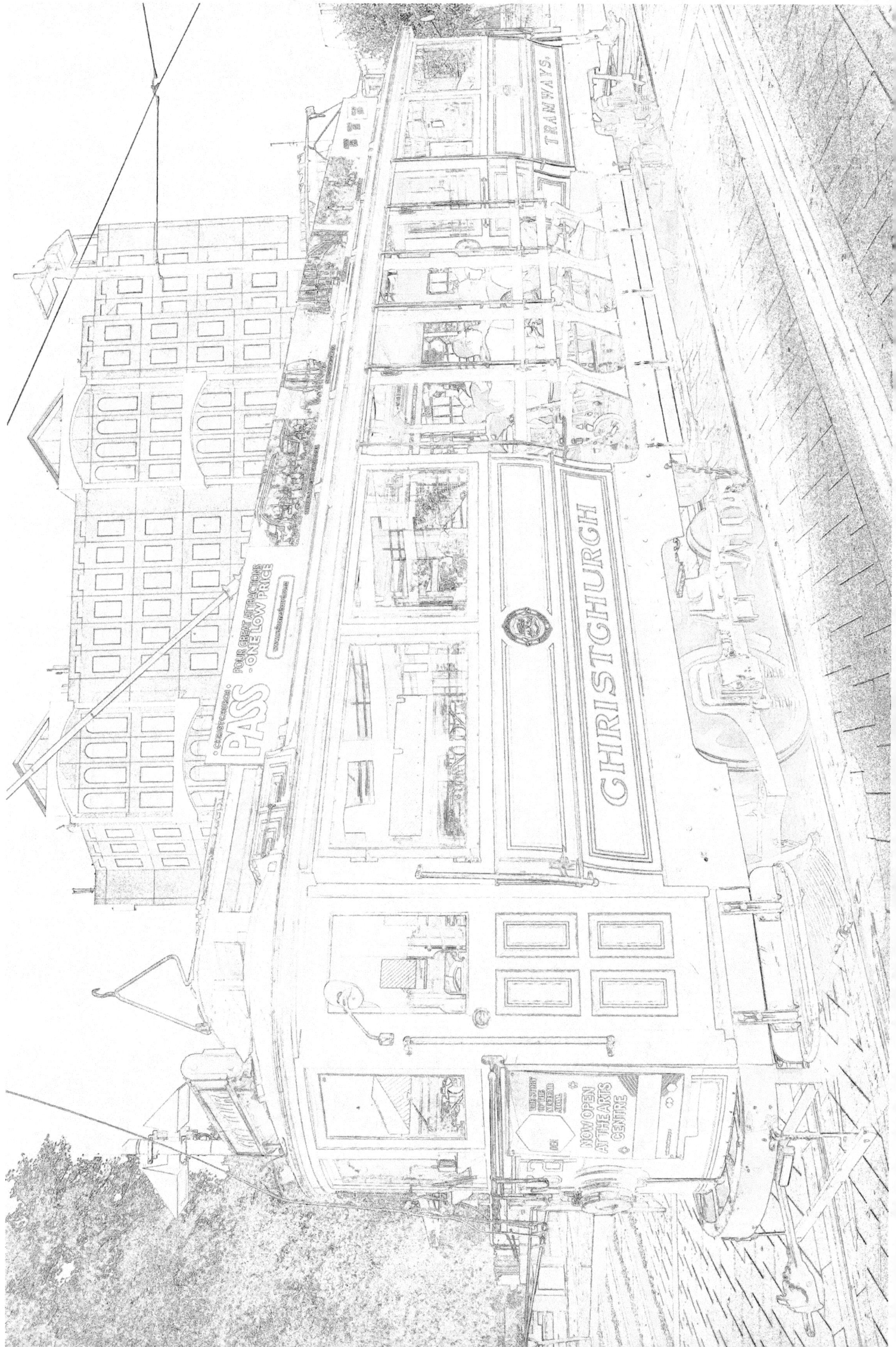
TRAMWAYS.
CHRISTCHURCH
PASS
FOUR GREAT ATTRACTIONS
· ONE LOW PRICE
NOW OPEN
AT THE ARTS
CENTRE

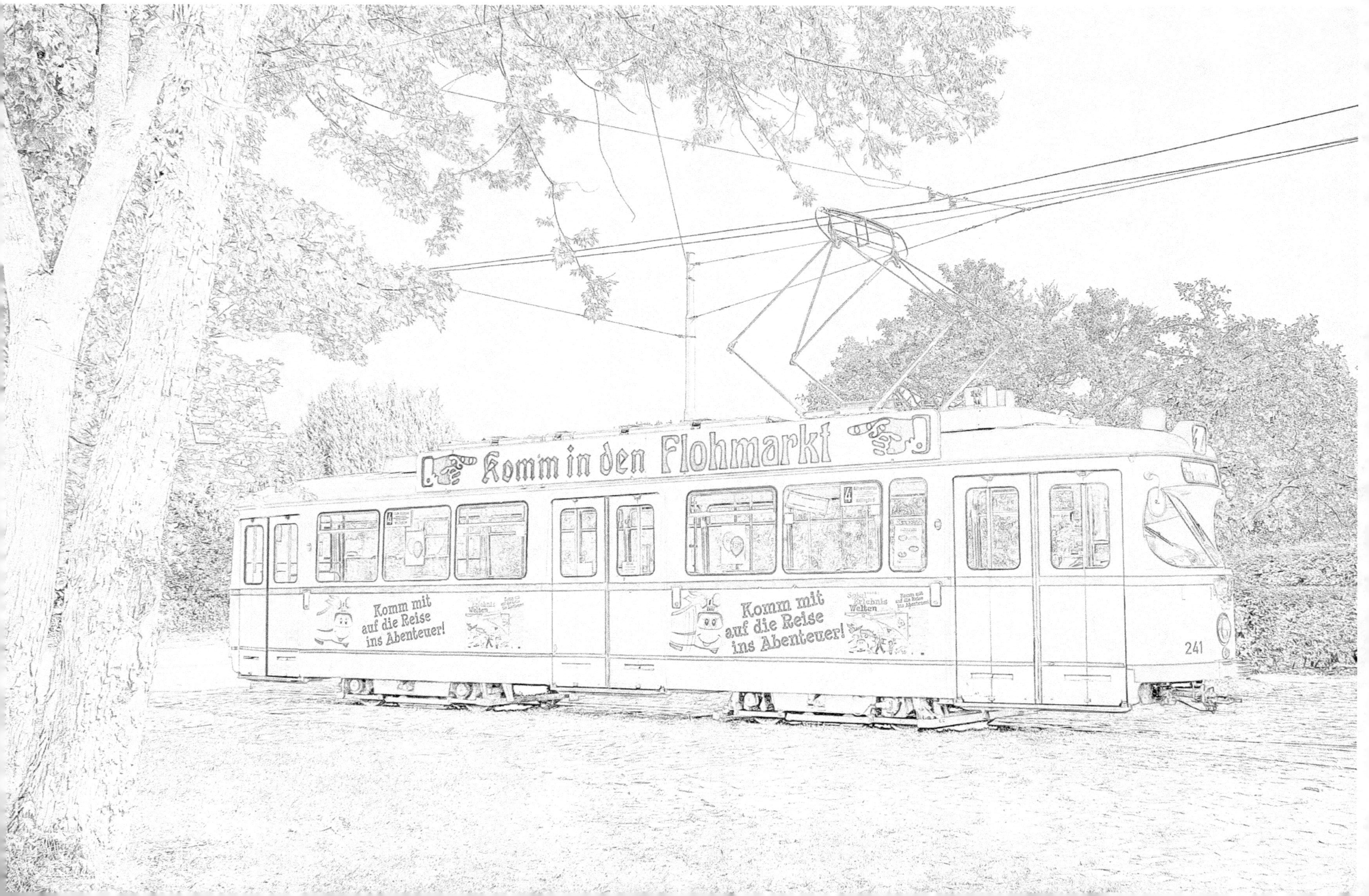
Komm in den Flohmarkt
Komm mit
auf die Reise
ins Abenteuer!
Komm mit
auf die Reise
ins Abenteuer!
241

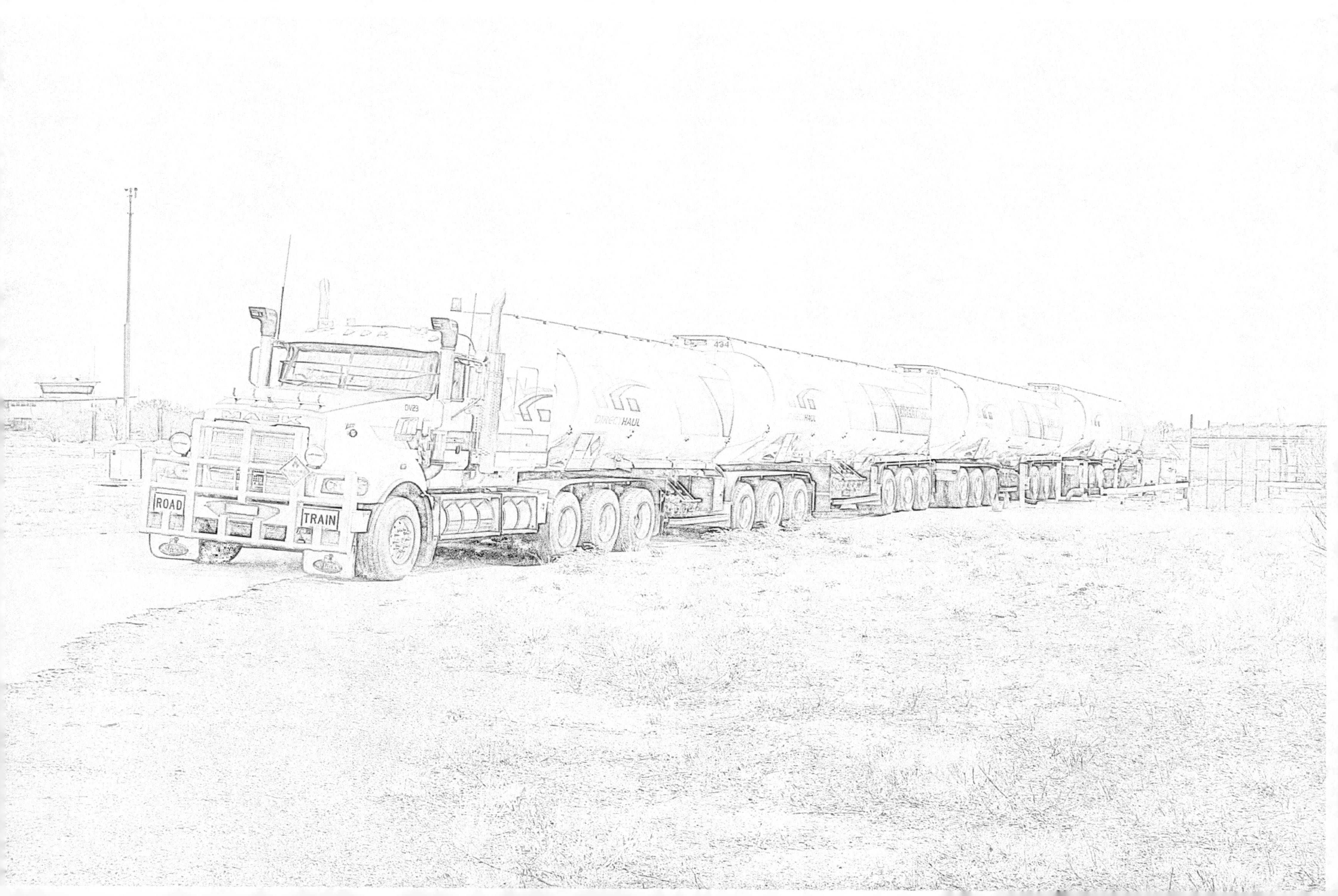
MACK
DV23
ROAD
TRAIN
DIRECTHAUL
434
435

www.ingramcontent.com/pod-product-compliance
Lightning Source LLC
Chambersburg PA
CBHW081056180526
45170CB00005B/1779